50 POWER PRAYERS FROM SCRIPTURE FOR YOU - VERSES AND PRAYER SIDE-BY-SIDE

Gratitude Encouragement Strength Guidance (Classic Cover with Cross)

LEE KOWAL, MDIV

KINGDOM
LIFE
BOOKS™

COPYRIGHT

Kingdom Life Books_{TM}

50 POWER PRAYERS FROM SCRIPTURE FOR YOU - Verses and Prayer Side-by-Side

Gratitude Encouragement Strength Guidance (Classic Cover with Cross)

'Send inquiries to: Kingdom Life Books, PO Box 4, Lincoln City, Oregon 97367

www.KingdomLifeBooks.com

Paperback © November 2018 ISBN: 9781949261172

PRAYER BOOK TABLE OF CONTENTS

Part 10
PRAYERS IN SCRIPTURE

Part 11
MORNING & EVENING PRAYERS

Part 12
POWERFUL PRAYERS IN ANCIENT HYMNIC POETRY

50 POWER PRAYERS & SCRIPTURE

with MOMENTS OF GRATITUDE

...True prayer is measured by weight, not by length.
A single groan before God may have more fullness
of prayer in it than a fine oration of great length.
- C. H. Spurgeon

CALLED "50 POWER PRAYERS" BECAUSE THEY STAND SIDE BY SIDE WITH SCRIPTURE VERSES UPON WHICH THEY ARE BUILT!

*T*his personal prayerbook includes written prayers that do not hinder spiritual engagement or replace personal prayers, but rather they provide spiritual fuel to engage mind & heart, to stimulate your conversation with God. Moment of gratitude end prayers with uplift.

"For the word of God is alive and active..."

—HEBREWS 4:12

Prayers arranged thematically for ease:
Comfort - Love - Strength - Gratitude - Peace - Joy - Guidance

Also included:
7 Days of Mornings & Evenings
The Lord's Prayer Expanded
Prayers in Beloved Scripture
Prayers in Ancient Hymnic Poetry
Prayer for Salvation

REVITALIZE YOUR DEVOTIONAL PRAYER WHEN WORDS DON'T SEEM TO COME.

~ And renew your spiritual journey & friendship with God!

LET THESE PRAYERS ENERGIZE AND EDIFY YOUR PERSONAL PRAYER LIFE. Renew your relationship with God by opening the door with rich focused prayers that will engage your spirit with His in holy communion and intimacy!

Prayers that provide comfort during trials,
Encouragement when you need it,
A joyful uplift of spirit, just because you desire it!

The Lord is near to all who call upon Him,
To all who call upon Him in truth.

—PSALM 145:18

✝ ✝ ✝

REFOCUS – STATEMENT OF FAITH

*I*n the busyness and distractions of our daily schedule, reciting basic foundational beliefs can help turn our fragmented spirits from hectic world demands unto our solid Rock upon which we stand firm, to stabilize our priorities and revitalize our spirit by focusing on what truly matters, our true treasure:

Joy in our relationship with God and the peace of His Holy Spirit.

✝ ✝ ✝

FAITH STATEMENT —BASED ON THE APOSTLES CREED

I believe in God, the Father Almighty, Maker of heaven and earth.

I believe in Jesus Christ, His only Son, our Lord, who was conceived by the Holy Spirit, born of the virgin Mary, suffered under Pontius Pilate, was crucified, died and was buried. The third day He rose again from the dead. He ascended into heaven and sits at the right hand of God the Father Almighty. From thence He will come to judge the living and the dead. I believe in the Holy Spirit, the holy Christian Church, the communion of saints, the forgiveness of sins, the resurrection of the body, and the life everlasting. Amen.

✞ ✞ ✞

EXPANDED FAITH STATEMENT —BASED ON THE NICENE CREED

I BELIEVE IN ONE GOD, THE FATHER ALMIGHTY, MAKER OF HEAVEN AND earth, of all things visible and invisible.

I believe in one Lord Jesus Christ, the only begotten Son of God, born of the Father before all ages. God from God, Light from Light, true God from true God, begotten, not made, consubstantial with the Father; through Him all things were made. For us and for our salvation He came down from heaven, and by the Holy Spirit was incarnate of the Virgin Mary, and became man. For our sake He was crucified under Pontius Pilate.

He suffered death and was buried, and rose again on the third day. He ascended into heaven and is seated at the right hand of the Father. He will come again in glory to judge the living and the dead and His kingdom will have no end.

I believe in the Holy Spirit, the Lord, the giver of life, who proceeds from the Father and the Son, Who with the Father and the Son is adored and glorified, Who has spoken through the prophets. I believe in one, holy, Christian Church. I confess one baptism for the forgiveness of sins and I look forward to the resurrection of the dead and the life of the world to come. Amen.

✞ ✞ ✞

Each time, before you intercede, be quiet first, and worship God in His glory. Think of what He can do, and how He delights to hear the prayers of His redeemed people. Think of your place and privilege in Christ, and expect great things!

— ***ANDREW MURRAY***

HEAVENLY FATHER, PREPARE MY HEART TODAY AS I COME BEFORE YOUR throne in holy prayer, seeking to follow Your guidance, to grow spiritually in Christ's likeness, and to walk nearer to You than ever before. I long to experience that friendship and intimacy with You that brings joy and peace. The closer I am to You the greater my delight! Guard my mind and heart as I pursue You in my quiet devotional time I so long to please You.

In Jesus' Mighty Name. Amen.

PRAYERS FOR GUIDANCE

*Prayer does not fit us for the greater work;
prayer is the greater work.*
—Oswald Chambers

*In prayer it is better to have a heart without
words than words without a heart.*
—John Bunyan

GUIDE MY WAYS, LORD

Our Great Shepherd Leads us

Oh, that the Lord would guide my ways
To keep His statutes still!
Oh, that my God would grant me grace
To know and do His will!

...

Order my foot steps by Thy word
And make my heart sincere;
Let sin have no dominion, Lord,
But keep my conscience clear.

...

Assist my soul, too apt to stray,
A stricter watch to keep;
And should I e'er forget Thy way,
Restore Thy wand'ring sheep.

...

Make me to walk in Thy commands
—Tis a delightful road—
Nor let my head, or heart, or hands,
Offend against my God.
—Isaac Watts, 1700's

1. PRAYER FOR GUIDANCE IN DAILY LIFE

PRAYERS FOR GUIDANCE

irect me in the path of your commands, for there I find delight. Turn my heart toward your statutes and not toward selfish gain. Turn my eyes away from worthless things; preserve my life according to your word...I gain understanding from your precepts; therefore I hate every wrong path. Your word is a lamp for my feet, a light on my path.
—PSALM 119:35-37;104-105 - NIV

Walk in a manner worthy of the Lord, to please Him in all respects, bearing fruit in every good work and increasing in the knowledge of God...Let the word of Christ richly dwell within you, with all wisdom teaching and admonishing one another with psalms and hymns and spiritual songs, singing with thankfulness in your hearts to God. —COLOSSIANS 1:10;3:16

Lead me in the right path, O LORD...Point out anything in me that offends you, and lead me along the path of everlasting life.
—PSALMS 5:8;139:24 - NLT

I am the vine, you are the branches; he who abides in Me

and I in him, he bears much fruit, for apart from Me you can do nothing. —JOHN 15:5

For in Him we live and move and exist...'For we also are His *children.'* —ACTS 17:28

PRAYER

Holy Father, I long to walk continuously on Your path, the path You have designed for my life—for peace, fulfillment, and true joy. As I live out this day, help me keep my eyes ever upon You; then my footsteps will remain faithfully in the principles of Your Word and in Your divine purposes.

Give me understanding to know what are my worthless activities, so that in turning from them, I may walk purely in Your will, and in the awareness of Your presence with me. Teach me what really matters in life. Fill me with Your wisdom to budget my time—to make "room" for daily quiet-time and intimacy with You in Your Word, for strength, peace, and love. 'Without You I can do nothing.'

Oh Lord, by Whose grace "I live and move and have my being," guide me through the coming days and weeks. Teach me to remain on Your pathway, to be thoughtful toward those I meet, to find joy and delight in Your Word, which alone can purify my heart.

Please help me to see more clearly Your guidance through Your Word and Holy Spirit. And above all, keep me abiding in Your divine love, which has reconciled me to You in Christ Jesus. Amen.

MOMENT OF GRATITUDE: Thank You for the precious gift of today! You made all things and hold them together moment by moment with Your Spirit.

I am humbled before Your awesomeness, and held warmly and securely in Your loving hands. I thank You for each minute and every breath. Childlike trust in You, and simplicity of spirit cause me to rejoice and be glad.

2. PRAYER FOR GUIDANCE DURING TROUBLES

PRAYERS FOR GUIDANCE

"*I* *have come as Light into the world, so that everyone who believes in Me will not remain in darkness.*"
—John 12:46

When I sit in darkness, the Lord will be a light to me.
...In the multitude of my anxieties within me,
Your comforts delight my soul. —Micah 7:8; Psalm 94:19 - NKJ

"When you pass through the waters, I will be with you; And through the rivers, they will not overflow you. When you walk through the fire, you will not be scorched, Nor will the flame burn you. For I am the LORD your God,
The Holy One of Israel, your Savior." —Isaiah 43:2-3

Even though I walk through the valley of the shadow of death, I fear no evil: for You are with me; Your rod and Your staff they comfort me. —Psalm 23:4

The LORD is my light and my salvation; whom shall I fear?
The LORD is the strength of my life; of whom shall I be afraid?
—Psalm 27:1 - KJV

"I have told you these things, so that in me you may have peace. In this world you will have trouble. But take heart!
I have overcome the world." —John 16:33 - NIV

For thus the Lord GOD, the Holy One of Israel, has said,
"...In quietness and trust is your strength." —Isaiah 30:15

Prayer

Jesus, my Heavenly King and Loving Shepherd, I am ever comforted by Your guiding staff and Your rod of protection. You taught that in this life we will have trials, but that You have overcome them all and we have peace resting under Your protection, power, and provision. The dark places of the earth can feel like a flood of waters overtaking me, and as fire to hurt and destroy. But though the world around me is darkened, I remain safe, resting in You.

I am so very thankful to have You as the light in my life. Be ever my hope in the storm and my rock when the road before me is rough. You are my hiding place—I have no other refuge in this hour of darkness.

As I stand firmly in faith, take me through every dark circumstance safely. I confess there are times when I sense loss or danger, that anxiety and fear take hold of my heart. Ever remind me these feelings are not from You, to let go of unbelief and take hold of Your promises with a calm mind. Help me grab hold of these promises today with confident assurance—almighty Redeemer and Friend!

Let every difficult circumstance help me grow spiritually, closer in relationship with You, being evermore able to bear Your eternal fruit.(John 15:1-12) Remove worries and anxious fears, and give me grace to trust in You completely, and let Your Word ever be my guide in trying situations. I place my confidence in You and Your eternal love. Thank You for delighting my soul with comfort. Amen.

Moment of Gratitude: Thank You for using circumstances to strengthen my spiritual endurance and patience, and also my ability to care for others. Most of all, for showing me my complete and utter dependency on You! Even in difficulties, I am grateful to seek and find the treasure of Your presence with me through it all!

3. PRAYER TO WALK IN NEW LIFE

PRAYERS FOR GUIDANCE

W ALK IN NEW LIFE:
Therefore we have been buried with Him through baptism into death, so that as Christ was raised from the dead through the glory of the Father, so we too might walk in newness of life...

Therefore as you have received Christ Jesus the Lord, so walk in Him, having been firmly rooted and now being built up in Him and established in your faith, just as you were instructed, and overflowing with gratitude. —ROMANS 6:4; COLOSSIANS 2:6-7

Walk by the Spirit, and you will not gratify the desires of the flesh. For the desires of the flesh are against the Spirit, and the desires of the Spirit are against the flesh, for these are opposed to each other...
—GALATIANS 5:16-17 - ESV

If you have been raised up with Christ, keep seeking the things above, where Christ is, seated at the right hand of God. Set your mind on the things above, not on the things that are on earth.

For you have died and your life is hidden with Christ in God.
—COLOSSIANS 3:1-3

PRAYER

Help me walk today with a mindset of "seeking the things above"—seeking You. To walk so close to You that all my thoughts are in continuous dialogue with Your Spirit, to hear clearly Your Spirit's "still small voice".

Jesus, my heart-cry is to live each day worthy of Your calling! So many opportunities—bearing Your eternal fruit, learning more of You in Your Word, worshiping You. And as You taught, *'God is Spirit, and those who worship Him must worship in spirit and in truth'*.
—JOHN 4:24

I confess that walking in my spirit along with Your Spirit is challenging in this world that offers continuous satisfaction in every sort of "perceived as necessary" physical desire. Give me clear vision to see this deception and let go.

Since my life is hidden in You, please let me know if there is anything I hang on to that prevents me from living in Your fullness. I know if I abide with You in vital relationship, I will also find all things that relate to a joyful life.(PSALM 16:11) I ask that You help me die to myself so that I may truly live! This is my desire, but in the difficulty and busyness of life, I lose sight of Your path, distracted by self-satisfactions. Strengthen my walk in You and the awareness of Your presence with me every moment. Amen.

MOMENT OF GRATITUDE: Once again, Father, I thank You for directing my path into this new life with You. Thank You for pulling me away from the fruitless life of endless activities focused on self, that ultimately do not satisfy.

The truth of my new life, hidden in Your glorious loving arms, fills me with unexplainable gratitude. Lift me up to Your heart, and breathe upon me with Your Holy Spirit. Amen.

4. PRAYER TO WALK IN WAYS OF WISDOM

PRAYERS FOR GUIDANCE

*T*he fear of the LORD is the beginning of wisdom; all who follow his precepts have good understanding. To him belongs eternal praise...Teach us to number our days, that we may gain a heart of wisdom. —Psalms 111:10;90:12 - NIV
If any of you lacks wisdom, let him ask of God, who gives to all generously and without reproach, and it will be given to him. —James 1:5

Lead me in the right path, O Lord.
—Psalm 5:8 - NLT

The wise in heart will be called understanding,
And sweetness of speech increases persuasiveness.
Understanding is a fountain of life to one who has it,
But the discipline of fools is folly.
The heart of the wise instructs his mouth
And adds persuasiveness to his lips.
Pleasant words are a honeycomb, Sweet to the soul
and healing to the bones. —Proverbs 16:21-24
Point out anything in me that offends you, and lead me along
the path of everlasting life. —Psalm 139:24 - NLT

Your words were found and I ate them, And Your words became *for me a joy and the delight of my heart; For I have been called by* *Your name, O Lord God of hosts.* —Jeremiah 15:16

Prayer Inspired by Proverbs 3:3-6

My Loving Father, I ask today to walk in Your wisdom. Please help me to let love and faithfulness never leave me; to bind them around my neck like a beautiful necklace—to write them on the tablet of my heart.

Then I will win favor and a good name in the sight of Yourself and others. Help me to ever trust in You with all my heart and lean not on my own understanding; and in all my ways submit to You, and You will direct my life's pathway, making it straight before me!

Prayer

Oh Lord, I so desire to be wise of heart, to walk in the way that is following close behind You. I know this is the "right path" that You have ordained for me. I may not see this path clearly, but I am confident that as long as I keep my eyes focused sharply on You I will remain close behind You, and You will lead me in it!

Reveal anything in my mind and heart that offends You. And help me turn away from those things so I can see You more clearly.

By Your Holy Spirit, help me keep my speech sweet, and my heart full of instruction from Your Word. There is where my joy is full and I am strengthened by Your Spirit for that path You have divinely placed before me! Amen.

Moment of Gratitude: Thank You for showing me the ways of true wisdom in Scripture. It is a delightful path full of incomprehensible serenity, joy, love, and daily renewal. These are the mysteries hidden from the beginning of time, revealed to us in Your Son Jesus Christ, my Savior. I am eternally appreciative and glad!

PRAYERS TO KNOW GOD

To have God speak to the heart is a majestic experience, an experience that people may miss if they monopolize the conversation and never pause to hear God's responses.

—Charles Stanley

HELP ME KNOW YOU

Most merciful Redeemer, Friend and Brother,
may we know you more clearly,
love you more dearly,
and follow you more nearly,
day by day.
Amen.

—Prayer of St. Richard of Chichester

5. PRAYER TO KNOW GOD AS YOUR CREATOR

PRAYERS TO KNOW GOD

*O*UR UNSEEN CREATOR GOD IS SEEN ALL AROUND US: *For ever since the world was created, people have seen the earth and sky. Through everything God made, they can clearly see his invisible qualities—his eternal power and divine nature. So they have no excuse for not knowing God.*
—ROMANS 1:20 - NLT

In the beginning God created the heavens and the earth.
—GENESIS 1:1

By faith we understand that the entire universe was formed at God's command, that what we now see did not come from anything that can be seen. —HEBREWS 11:3 - NLT

The heavens are telling of the glory of God; And their expanse is declaring the work of His hands...O Lord, our Lord, How majestic is Your name in all the earth, Who have displayed Your splendor above the heavens...When I consider Your heavens, the work of Your fingers, The moon and the stars, which You have ordained; What is man that You take thought of him, And the son of man that You care for him?
—PSALMS 19:1;8:1,3-4

For your Creator will be your husband; the LORD of

Heaven's Armies is his name! He is your Redeemer, the Holy One of Israel, the God of all the earth. —Isaiah 54:5 - NLT
"I have loved you with an everlasting love: Therefore I have drawn you with lovingkindness." *—You formed my inward parts; You wove me in my mother's womb. I will give thanks to You, for I am fearfully and wonderfully made; Wonderful are Your works.* —Jeremiah 31:3; Psalm 139:13-14
LORD, make me to know my end; And what is the extent of my days; Let me know how transient I am. —Psalm 39:4
For God, who said, "Light shall shine out of darkness," is the One who has shone in our hearts to give the Light of the knowledge of the glory of God in the face of Christ. —2 Corinthians 4:6

Prayer

My almighty Creator and Lord, thank You for opening my eyes to see Your greatness in nature, animals, and people. Before You started the clock of time, You both knew me and desired a loving relationship with me—I feel loved! I praise you because I am fearfully and wonderfully made by Your glorious hands, by which You continue to hold me safely to this very day.

Please Lord, remind me how brief my time on earth will be. Remind me that my days are numbered, and how fleeting my life is, so I stay focused on Your will for my life. I humbly ask to know You more deeply as Creator God. My help, O Lord, comes from You, Who made heaven and earth! I lift up my joyful praise to You from Whom all blessings flow! my time, my life, my salvation, O mighty and merciful God are in Your hands. And to You I commit my body and soul for safekeeping in time and eternity! Let me ever bring praises to Your name as the most high, almighty Creator of all!

Moment of Gratitude: I overflow with gratitude for Your wonderful compassion, protection, and strength that accompanies me during my pilgrimage here on earth. And I thank You that, as I lie down and rest, Father and Creator of all, You keep me safe—on eagles' wings You carry and shelter me. O Lord, I love You dearly!

6. PRAYER TO KNOW HIS LOVE & COMPASSION

PRAYERS TO KNOW GOD

How precious also are Your thoughts to me, O God! How great is the sum of them! If I should count them, they would be more in number than the sand; When I awake, I am still with You.
—PSALM 139:17-18 - NKJ

The LORD's lovingkindnesses indeed never cease, For His compassions never fail. They are new every morning.
—LAMENTATIONS 3:22-23

I sat down under his shadow with great delight, and his fruit was sweet to my taste. He brought me to the banqueting house, and his banner over me was love. —SONG OF SOLOMON 2:3-4 - KJV

"Behold, My Servant, whom I uphold; My chosen one in whom My soul delights...He will not cry out or raise His voice, Nor make His voice heard in the street. A bruised reed He will not break And a dimly burning wick He will not extinguish; He will faithfully bring forth justice. —ISAIAH 42:1-3

But from there you will search again for the Lord your God. And if you search for him with all your heart and soul, you will find him..."Keep on asking, and you will receive what you ask for. Keep on seeking, and you will find. Keep on knocking, and the door will be opened to you. For everyone who asks, receives. Everyone

*who seeks, finds. And to everyone who knocks, the door will be
opened."* —Deuteronomy 4:29; Matthew 7:7-8 - NLT

Prayer Inspired by Ephesians 3:14-21

*F*or this reason, I bow my knees before You, oh Father, from whom every family in heaven and on earth derives its name, that You would grant me, according to the riches of Your glory, to be strengthened with power through Your Spirit in my inner-person, so that Christ may dwell in my heart through faith; and that I, being rooted and grounded in love, may be able to comprehend with all the saints what is the breadth and length and height and depth, and to know the love of Christ which surpasses knowledge, that I may be filled up to all the fullness of God.

Now to You, who are able to do farmore abundantly beyond all that I can ask or think, according to the power that works within me, to You be the glory in the church and in Christ Jesus to all generations forever and ever. Amen.

Prayer

Father of all creation, thank You for loving all people so much that You gave us a choice to love You back, and for saving us through Jesus. I feel secure and steadfast in Your love. Safe from grief, fear, and pain, hide me in You—my everlasting God!

Fasten my heart and hope in You, and let my strivings and desires be directed to the treasures of Your love. As long as I am in this land of pilgrimage, hold my hand; and increase my awareness of Your glorious presence keeping me every moment. Help me to make space and time to spend with You daily in Your Word, so that our friendship may grow in strength and love. In the name of Jesus Christ my Lord, Amen.

MOMENT OF GRATITUDE: I am overjoyed as I ponder the grace of learning of, and living in the depths of Your eternal love. I am forever thankful that I will be ever finding new indescribable "gems" in Your holy treasury of love!

7. PRAYER TO KNOW HIM AS YOUR PROTECTOR

PRAYERS TO KNOW GOD

*T*hose who live in the shelter of the Most High will find* rest in the shadow of the Almighty. This I declare about the LORD: He alone is my refuge, my place of safety; he is my God, and I trust him. For he will rescue you from every trap and protect you from deadly disease. He will cover you with his feathers. He will shelter you with his wings. His faithful promises are your armor and protection. Do not be afraid of the terrors of the night, nor the arrow that flies in the day. Do not dread the disease that stalks in darkness, nor the disaster that strikes at midday.* —PSALMS 91:1-6 - NLT

Though a thousand fall at your side, though ten thousand are dying around you, these evils will not touch you. —If you make the LORD your refuge, if you make the Most High your shelter, no evil will conquer you; no plague will come near your home. For he will order his angels to protect you wherever you go. They will hold you up with their hands so you won't even hurt your foot on a stone. —PSALM 91:7, 9-12 - NLT

The LORD says, "I will rescue those who love me. I will protect those who trust in my name. When they call on me, I will answer; I will be with them in trouble. I will rescue and honor them." —PSALM 91:14-15 - NLT

Have mercy on me, O God, have mercy! I look to you for protection. *I will hide beneath the shadow of your wings until the danger passes by. I cry out to God Most High, to God who will fulfill his purpose for me. He will send help from heaven to rescue me, disgracing those who hound me. My God will send forth his unfailing love and faithfulness.* —PSALM 57:1-3 - NLT

Neither height nor depth, nor anything else in all creation, will be able to separate us from the love of God that is in Christ Jesus our Lord. —ROMANS 8:39 - NIV

PRAYER

Heavenly Father, with praise and joy I look up to You as the Helper and Deliverer who has heard my prayers. I am Your child and You dwell in my heart. Living so intimately with each other, I also know that I dwell in the safety of Your presence that covers me. Fasten my heart and hope in You.

I realize that focusing on "issues" only serves to diminish my faith and cause fear. The pressures of life sometimes cause me to feel paralyzed, not knowing where to turn. So I ask by the power of Your Holy Spirit, please turn my eyes completely away from my situation and myself. Point them firmly on Your almighty loving care that You are providing for me this very moment, this day, and into eternity.

Keep me safe from all threats of sickness, loss, and hardship. In obedience and faith, with the help of Your Holy Spirit, I will be at peace by placing my complete trust and reliance on You as my almighty protector and Savior Who cares for me as a loving shepherd. I ask that You complete the purpose You have for my life, and keep me ever under Your shadow of unfailing love and faithfulness.

MOMENT OF GRATITUDE: Thank You for fighting for me and for giving me armor needed to stand against the dark forces of the enemy (Ephesians 6:10-18). It is You Who protects me. I am grateful that You continue to walk with me, clothing me in Your love and protection today and everyday day. Amen.

8. PRAYER TO KNOW HIS STRENGTH

PRAYERS TO KNOW GOD

he joy of the Lord is your strength. —Nehemiah 8:10

The LORD is the everlasting God, the Creator of the ends of the earth. *He will not grow tired or weary, and his understanding no one can fathom. He gives strength to the weary and increases the power of the weak…those who hope in the Lord will renew their strength. They will soar on wings like eagles; they will run and not grow weary, they will walk and not be faint.*
—Isaiah 40:28-31 - NIV

The Lord is my strength and my shield; My heart trusts in Him, *and I am helped; Therefore my heart exults, And with my song I shall thank Him…The Lord will give strength to His people; The Lord will bless His people with peace.* —Psalms 28:7;29:11

God is our strength

LORD, you are my strength and fortress, my refuge in the day of *trouble!…God remains the strength of my heart; he is mine forever.*
—Jeremiah 16:19; Psalm 73:26 - NLT

You are the salt of the earth. But what good is salt if it has lost *its flavor? Can you make it salty again? It will be thrown out and* *trampled underfoot as worthless. You are the light of the world—like a city on a hilltop that cannot be hidden. No one lights a lamp and then puts it under a basket. Instead, a lamp is placed on a stand, where it gives light to everyone in the house. In the same way, let your good deeds shine out for all to see, so that everyone will praise your heavenly Father.* —MATTHEW 5:13-16 - NLT

PRAYER

My Lord, Help me to always remember that You created everything and so You are the most powerful and able person to take care of me! Oh heavenly Father, Your strength is my joy and peace—my foundation in life and my hope! I can fully trust in both Your ability and willingness to strengthen me when I feel weak emotionally, or physically.

You are my caretaker in this life, and I daily need to be renewed in Your strength, to be filled afresh with your supernatural power to overcome each obstacle in my path. With my eyes on you, Lord, hand in hand, You working through me, I can make it.

Thank You, Lord, that Your joy will completely consume the weakness of my life and make me strong again—filling all the tired parts of my heart and mind exceedingly and abundantly!

Father, my sincere desire is for greater strength and spiritual growth, the kind of growth that brings me into a vibrantly close and strong relationship with You, and growth to bear Your fruit. Please give health, courage, and confidence in my work this day, that I may prove to be salt and a light to my neighbors, and to fearlessly confess my faith in Jesus Christ, my Redeemer. I commit myself into Your loving hands, Father, Son, and Holy Spirit!

MOMENT OF GRATITUDE: Oh, most gracious heavenly Father, You are the mightiest power of all, and yet You care about and strengthen even the most insignificant areas of my heart and mind—and for this I thank You.

PRAYERS TO LOVE GOD & OTHERS

A Christian should always remember that the value of his good works is not based on their number and excellence, but on the love of God which prompts him to do these things.
—JUAN DE LA CRUZ
(SAINT JOHN OF THE CROSSS)

Whatever a person may be like, we must still love them because we love God.
—JOHN CALVIN

HELP ME LOVE YOU AND OTHERS

Through love serve one another. —Galatians 5:13

My soul with grateful thoughts of love
Entirely is possess'd,
Because the Lord vouchsafed to hear
The voice of my request.
Since He has now His ear inclined,
I never will despair;
But still in each event of life
To Him address my prayer.

—AUTHOR UNKOWN, 18TH CENTURY
(INSPIRED BY PSALM 116)

9. PRAYER FOR OUR LOVE FOR GOD

*T*eacher, which is the greatest commandment in the Law? Jesus replied: "'Love the Lord your God with all your heart and with all your soul and with all your mind. This is the first and greatest commandment."...Your name is like perfume poured out...Let my beloved come into his garden and taste its choice fruits.* —Matthew 22:36-38; Song of Solomon 1:3; 4:16 - NIV

O love the LORD, all you His godly ones! —Psalm 31: 23

Therefore, to you who believe, He is precious...We love Him *because He first loved us.* —1 Peter 2:7; 1 John 4:19 - NKJ

And His name will be called Wonderful...and His name is *called The Word of God...And has on His robe and on His thigh He has a name written, KING OF KINGS, AND LORD OF LORDS.* —Isaiah 9:6; Revelation 19:13,16 - NKJ

No one can serve two masters. For you will hate one and *love the other; you will be devoted to one and despise the other. You cannot serve God and be enslaved to money.* —Matthew 6:24 - NLT

Show we Love God Through Obedience: **"And walk in love, just as Christ also loved you and gave Himself up for us,** *an offering and a sacrifice to God as a fragrant aroma."...* "If you love Me you will keep my commandments." —Ephesians 5:2; John 14:15

JESUS EXAMPLE OF SPENDING TIME WITH OUR FATHER:
Very early in the morning, while it was still dark, Jesus got up, left the house and went off to a solitary place, where he prayed.
—MARK 1:35 - NIV

You will seek Me and find Me when you search for Me with all your heart. —JEREMIAH 29:13

PRAYER

Father of all creation, Your love fills me with great delight—I find all-encompassing warmth and contentment in Your loving arms.

I pray that Your Spirit rest upon me as I ponder Your great love for me this day. I am so very thankful that You have blessed me with the ability to feel Your loving compassion. It gives me confidence to walk through this day and week knowing I am not alone.

I submit myself to Your care and love. I can only know what true love is by learning from You...Please show me *how* to love You with all my heart, as my highest priority. I long to be fully obedient to You.

At times it is hard for me to sacrifice my rights to either justify myself or deny others love because of fear. Grant me strength to submit to Your love. Help me to become ever more aware of Your loving presence through every minute of each day, to love You aright in my spirit, and in truth!

Things that seem urgent tend to take precedence in my life. Help me simplify my life to make space for You, to be in Your presence, to know and love You in truth. When I do place a higher priority on seeking "things" than seeking communion with You, please forgive me. And as Jesus taught how important it is to intentionally make time to be in intimate company with You, I too wish to do the same more earnestly. Help me gain that life lived in friendship with You, so I may love You fully, my Lord and King.

MOMENT OF GRATITUDE: The greatest gift I have ever known is the awareness of Your love for me! The reality of You in my life fills my heart with humble gratitude and thanksgiving; I am now able to face each day contented in Your extreme peace and joy.

10. PRAYER FOR LOVE OF ONE ANOTHER–1

PRAYERS TO LOVE GOD & OTHERS

*W*alk in a manner worthy of the calling to which you *have been called, with all humility and gentleness, with patience, bearing with one another in love, eager to maintain the unity of the Spirit in the bond of peace.* —Ephesians 4:1-3 - ESV

May the Lord make your love increase and overflow for each other and for everyone else, just as ours does for you. May he strengthen your hearts so that you will be blameless and holy in the presence of our God and Father when our Lord Jesus comes with all his holy ones…Now about your love for one another we do not need to write to you, for you yourselves have been taught by God to love each other.
—1 Thessalonians 3:12-13; 4:9 - NIV

Beloved, let us love one another, for love is of God; and everyone who loves is born of God and knows God. He who does not love does not know God, for God is love… Beloved, if God so loved us, we also ought to love one another. No one has seen God at any time. If we love one another, God abides in us, and His love has been perfected

in us. By this we know that we abide in Him, and He in us, because He has given us of His Spirit.
—1 JOHN 4:7-8;11-13 - NKJ

Let no debt remain outstanding, except the continuing debt to love one another, for whoever loves others has fulfilled the law.
—ROMANS 13:8 - NIV

PRAYER

Heavenly Father, I stand humbly before You asking to know You more intimately—that I may also know Your love more fully, to love others completely, and display Your love to the world.

I ask that Your Spirit will guide me in loving others. As You are the author of love I ask for You to teach me how—help me focus my eyes firmly on You throughout the day, so that I will be consciously aware of Your leading. Help me sacrifice my time for the sake of spending it alone with You in Scripture because as I become firmly rooted in You, my love will increase and overflow! (Ephesians 3:14-21)

Help me to walk in the purity of Your love so I may shine the light of Your love to others. Show me how I may express gratitude in a unique way to someone in my life.

Lead me to those who need to feel Your love through me. Give me courage to freely share the new life You offer to them, and the wisdom to listen and speak those words You provide, in the moment You provide them. (Matthew 10:19)

Cleanse my heart of all ill will toward those I encounter during my daily life. Please show me any area of my heart that I need to submit more fully to You, or whether there are things I need to eliminate, to free up time for "Your love". I truly desire that Your loving light may shine more brightly through me.

MOMENT OF GRATITUDE: Thank You for giving us, Your church, the freedom to worship together, to gather together in Your name. And thank You for our Pastor and church staff. Bless them with integrity and wisdom and guide them as they lead us to further Your loving Gospel in this world.

11. PRAYER FOR LOVE OF ONE ANOTHER—2

PRAYERS TO LOVE GOD & OTHERS

THEY'LL KNOW WE ARE CHRISTIANS BY OUR LOVE:
"A new command I give you: Love one another.
As I have loved you, so you must love one another. By this everyone will know that you are my disciples, if you love one another." —JOHN 13:34-35 - NIV

Beloved, let us love one another, for love is from God,
and whoever loves has been born of God and knows God.
Anyone who does not love does not know God,
because God is love.

—1 JOHN 4:7-8

Let us hold unswervingly to the hope we profess, for he who *promised is faithful. And let us consider how we may spur one another on toward love and good deeds, not giving up meeting together, as some are in the habit of doing,but encouraging one another—and all the more as you see the Day approaching.*
—HEBREWS 10:23-25 - NIV

Having purified your souls by your obedience to the truth for a
sincere brotherly love, love one another earnestly from a pure heart,
since you have been born again, not of perishable seed but of
imperishable, through the living and abiding word of God.
—1 PETER 1:22-23 - ESV

PRAYER

My Loving Father, Lord, help me be a conduit of Your love and give me a heart that fully seeks to fulfill Your call to love.

Holy Lord, in the busyness of my life I find myself drifting from the "walk" You have designed for me. Give me wisdom to slow down, so I may show all forms of kindness with a peaceful spirit in the strength You provide, not my own—especially to those in the household of faith. The world should see that You are a God of love by observing how we, Your Church, love each other.

Help me, oh Lord, to see that I need other believers and they also need me. With a solid faith in Your hope, I ask for a renewed sense of commitment to help others in their faith! I ask for a spirit of love and truth.

Remove my fleshly tendencies to control or complain. Help me eliminate everything that inhibits me from fulfilling this calling. Help me feel the joy of relationships within Your family.

Holy Lord, Your eternal Word washes me clean from everything that stands in our way of seeing, hearing, and following You in the path of Your love. Encourage me to be even more diligent to read, study, and obey Your truth, and to love in purity.

Preserve me in my trials. When others seem to be against me, You give my heart strength and hope. I worship You, Almighty King! In the name of my loving Savior, Jesus Christ. Amen.

MOMENT OF GRATITUDE: I express my gratitude to You, that Your Spirit guides me in loving others. Thank You for not leaving me alone as I walk this path of life on earth. I love You!

PRAYERS FOR COMFORT

*God speaks in the silence of the heart.
Listening is the beginning of prayer.*

—MOTHER TERESA

SEND COMFORT LORD

What a friend we have in Jesus, all our sins and griefs to bear!
What a privilege to carry, everything to God in prayer!
O what peace we often forfeit, O what needless pain we bear,
all because we do not carry, everything to God in prayer!
...
Have we trials and temptations? Is there trouble anywhere?
We should never be discouraged; take it to the Lord in prayer!
Can we find a friend so faithful, who will all our sorrows share?
Jesus knows our every weakness; take it to the Lord in prayer!
...
Are we weak and heavy laden, cumbered with a load of care?
Precious Savior, still our refuge—take it to the Lord in prayer!
Do your friends despise, forsake you? Take it to the Lord in prayer!
In his arms he'll take and shield you; you will find a solace there.

—JOSEPH MEDLICOTT SCRIVEN, 1855

(INSPIRED BY MATTHEW 21:22, JOHN 15:15)

12. PRAYER FOR COMFORT FROM THE HOLY SPIRIT

PRAYERS FOR COMFORT

"*B*ut the Advocate, the Holy Spirit, whom the Father will* send in my name, will teach you all things and will remind you of everything I have said to you. Peace I leave with you; my peace I give you. I do not give to you as the world gives. Do not let your hearts be troubled and do not be afraid."
—JOHN 14:26-27 - NIV

"But when he, the Spirit of truth, comes, he will guide you *into all the truth. He will not speak on his own; he will speak only what he hears, and he will tell you what is yet to come. He will glorify me because it is from me that he will receive what he will make known to you.*" —JOHN 16:13-14 - NIV

When my anxious thoughts multiply within me, Your *consolations delight my soul.*
—PSALM 94:19

I pray for them...I will remain in the world no longer, but *they are still in the world...Holy Father, protect them by the power of your name...so that they may be one as we are one...I am coming to you now, but I say these things while I am still in the world, so that they may have the full measure of my joy within them.*
—JOHN 17:9,11,13 - NIV

Now, Israel, what does the Lord your God require from you, *but to fear the Lord your God, to walk in all His ways and love Him, and to serve the Lord your God with all your heart and with all your soul...The Lord is the one who goes ahead of you; He will be with you. He will not fail you or forsake you. Do not fear or be dismayed... Thus says the Lord,"Stand by the ways and see and ask for the ancient paths, where the good way is, and walk in it; And you will find rest for your souls."* —Deuteronomy 10:12;31:8; Jeremiah 6:16

Prayer

Holy Spirit, divine Comforter, sent into the world to give knowledge of God and understanding of heavenly things, give me a clearer and better understanding of the riches and the power of God, and of the way of life which is found in Christ Jesus, my Lord.

O Holy Spirit, make all things new in my life; make me truly reborn to God. Free me from every taint of the sinful flesh, and give me strength to conquer all temptations to sin, and all fears and doubts. Give me victory over every doubt and all dismay, all hatred and wickedness in the world, and bring rest and peace to my soul.

Through the power of Your indwelling, make me more perfect in following the ways of Jesus. Take full possession of my mind, and use me for Your purposes and service.

Most precious Spirit, be my everlasting Guide, in my pilgrimage here on earth and in that day when I travel to the city of God, which is in heaven. As You raised me from spiritual death to life in Christ and made me new, give me confidence and peace in Your salvation from bodily death to eternal life in the heavenly mansions. Spirit of God, give me a greater sense of Your life within me day after day. And with the Father and Son, make Your abode in me forevermore.

Moment of Gratitude: I am forever appreciative that You have gifted me with the Comforter, Intercessor, Advocate, Helper, and Strengthener, Who is with me always and forevermore—The Treasure of my heart.

I am safe and cared for. Gratitude consumes me, I love You.

13. PRAYER FOR COMFORT IN TIMES OF TROUBLE

PRAYERS FOR COMFORT

God blesses those who mourn, for they will be comforted. —He heals the brokenhearted and bandages their wounds. —Matthew 5:4; Psalm 147:3 - NLT

"When you pass through the waters, I will be with you;
And through the rivers, they will not overflow you.
When you walk through the fire, you will not be scorched,
Nor will the flame burn you. For I am the LORD your God,
The Holy One of Israel, your Savior." —Isaiah 43:2-3

Even though I walk through the valley of the shadow of death, I fear no evil, for You are with me; Your rod and Your staff, they comfort me. —Psalm 23:4
The LORD is my light and my salvation; whom shall I fear? The LORD is the strength of my life; of whom shall I be afraid? —Psalm 27:1 - KJV

"I have told you these things, so that in me you may have peace. In this world you will have trouble. But take heart! I have overcome the world." —John 16:33 - NIV
"But for you who fear my name, the Sun of Righteousness

will rise with healing in his wings. And you will go free, leaping with joy like calves let out to pasture. " —Malachi 4:2 - NLT

Jesus traveled throughout the region of Galilee, teaching in the synagogues and announcing the Good News about the Kingdom. And he healed every kind of disease and illness...Then Jesus said, "Come to me, all of you who are weary and carry heavy burdens, and I will give you rest...I am humble and gentle at heart, and you will find rest for your souls. "
—Matthew 4:23; 11:28-29 - NLT

Prayer

O Lord, eternal God, my Father in Christ Jesus, hear my prayer as I come to You in my trouble and distress. You are my hiding place. I have no other refuge in this hour my Lord, You can heal, repair, bind up, restore, and renew. In my anxious cares and troubles I come to You, trusting in Your holy Word and believing in Your promises.

You know that I have been greatly upset by the worries, fear, and doubts of the day. You must be my strength and refuge if I am to find peace of mind and healing. Uphold me with Your almighty arm. Give me grace to put all my trust in You. Let Your healing hand rest upon me day after day.

Let not the sufferings and cares of this day make me despondent. Teach me to believe that Your abiding presence will uphold me from hour to hour. Give me peaceful days and restful nights, bless me with refreshing sleep. Come to me with healing in Your wings. Speak to my soul the comforting promises of Your Word, and keep me steadfast in faith to the end. Bless all those around me and keep all of us cheerful, hopeful, and confident in You. I ask this of You, Who redeemed me with Your own blood. In the powerful name of Jesus, Amen.

Moment of Gratitude: Your healing balm brings joy and warmth to my soul! Thank You that I am able to supernaturally lay all my concerns down at Your feet, every burden, every care—letting go completely, trusting and resting in Your almighty loving arms!

14. PRAY TO COMFORT OTHERS IN DISTRESS

PRAYERS FOR COMFORT

*B*ut now, thus says the Lord, your Creator, O Jacob, *And He who formed you, O Israel, "Do not fear, for I have redeemed you; I have called you by name; you are Mine!*

When you pass through the waters, I will be with you; And through the rivers, they will not overflow you. When you walk through the fire, you will not be scorched, Nor will the flame burn you. For I am the LORD your God, The Holy One of Israel, your Savior. —Isaiah 43:1-3

The Lord is my shepherd; I have all that I need.
He lets me rest in green meadows;
he leads me beside peaceful streams...
Even when I walk through the darkest valley,
I will not be afraid, for you are close beside me.
Your rod and your staff protect and comfort me...
Surely your goodness and unfailing love
will pursue me all the days of my life,
and I will live in the house of the LORD forever.
—Psalm 23:1-2,4,6 - NLT

All praise to God, the Father of our Lord Jesus Christ.
God is our merciful Father and the source of all comfort.
He comforts us in all our troubles so that we can comfort others.
When they are troubled, we will be able to give them the same
comfort God has given us. For the more we suffer for Christ, the
more God will shower us with his comfort through Christ.
—2 Corinthians 1:3-5 - NLT

PRAYER

Comfort others with that same comfort you have received from God

We pray for those who grieve today. We ask for Your comfort to surround those who weep. We pray for the peace of Your presence to cover their minds and thoughts, even as You remind us that the enemy can never steal us out of Your hands; comfort them also with this same assurance that they are kept safe in Your presence forever, whether in life or in death.

Today, divine Shepherd of our souls, we pray that You embrace _____ (name of person in need) with Your love, and protect them throughout this day. They need You, they are wounded and bruised, sick at heart and in trouble and distress.

We come to You for their sake, in mercy and love uphold them amid their trial and tribulations. Strengthen their faith. Take every doubt out of their heart, and lead them into Your Holy Word where You promise to be with them always in every situation of life. Calm their nerves and put their mind at ease. Make them hopeful and patient. O Christ, have mercy on them. Be with them now and forevermore.

Help us to continue making space and time to spend alone with You daily, so that our relationship with You may grow in strength and love—to fully experience Your comfort so we may confidently extend it to others. Amen.

MOMENT OF GRATITUDE: You have promised that, as long as we are in this land of our pilgrimage, You will be our Shepherd; We are so very thankful that You have shown us loving care and compassion and have increased our awareness of Your glorious presence, keeping us every moment.

PRAYERS FOR PEACE

The Lord bless you, and keep you;
The Lord make His face shine on you,
And be gracious to you;
The Lord lift up His countenance on you,
And give you peace.

—Numbers 6:24-26

SEND PEACE LORD

When peace like a river attendeth my way,
when sorrows like sea billows roll;
whatever my lot, thou hast taught me to say,
"It is well, it is well with my soul."

...

Though Satan should buffet, though trials should come,
let this blest assurance control:
that Christ has regarded my helpless estate,
and has shed his own blood for my soul.

—HORATIO GATES SPAFFORD, 1873

15. PRAYER FOR THE PEACE OF GOD

PRAYERS FOR PEACE

F or God is not a God of confusion but of peace.
—1 CORINTHIANS 14:33

But now in Christ Jesus you who once were far away have been brought near by the blood of Christ. For he himself is our peace. —EPHESIANS 2:13-14 - NIV

"I will ask the Father, and He will give you another Helper,
that He may be with you forever; that is the Spirit of truth…
you know Him because He abides with you and will be in you…
the Helper, the Holy Spirit, whom the Father will
send in My name, He will teach you all things,
and bring to your remembrance all that I said to you.
Peace I leave with you; My peace I give to you;
not as the world gives do I give to you.
Do not let your heart be troubled, nor let it be fearful."
—JOHN 14:16,17,26-27

Now may the Lord of peace Himself continually
grant you peace in every circumstance…
Peace from Him who is and who was and who is to come.
—2 THESSALONIANS 3:16; REVELATIONS 1:4

The Lord will give strength to His people; The Lord will bless His people with peace...Depart from evil and do good; Seek peace and pursue it...But the meek shall inherit the earth, And shall delight themselves in the abundance of peace...Mercy and truth have met together; Righteousness and peace have kissed.
—PSALMS 29:11; 34:14; 37:11; 85:10 - NKJ

"These things I have spoken to you, so that in Me you may have peace. In the world you have tribulation, but take courage; I have overcome the world." —JOHN 16:33

PRAYER

My Lord, There is no true peace in pleasures apart from You. Jesus, You are my resting place, I find peace and serenity in You.

It is the temporary worldly "seemingly okay" pleasures that tend to pull me away from Your Spirit, Your true life, and Your true peace. Help me to discern the difference. I yield my control, and let go of everything I am trying to fix, handing it over to You.

After having experienced Your peace that passes all understanding, I now see that the busy chaos of accumulating "things" and trying to find fulfillment elsewhere has me in turmoil. Now I see that these things only distract me from the awareness of Your presence—and true, deep, abiding peace. Guide my steps in submission to Your continuous abiding love, to stop searching for worldly solutions, to live fully in You.

Lord, I see that true peace comes from You as a gift, and that rule will not change for all eternity. I know that I cannot do anything in my own efforts to acquire the peaceful countenance that only comes from You. Whenever I'm stressed, anxious, or afraid, help me remember to run to You. You're the only one that can calm my fears and end my fretful behavior.

MOMENT OF GRATITUDE: I am so thankful, Lord, that You offer peace to us as a generous gift, and that You freely give it to those who enter into relationship with You. I give thanks to You for that peace and also give You my heart as I gladly receive Your peace in faith. Thank You my Lord Jesus, You are my all in all. Amen

16. PRAYER FOR PEACE OF MIND

PRAYERS FOR PEACE

*D*on't worry about anything; instead, pray about everything. Tell God what you need, and thank him for all he has done. Then you will experience God's peace, which exceeds anything we can understand. His peace will guard your hearts and minds as you live in Christ Jesus…Fix your thoughts on what is true, and honorable, and right, and pure, and lovely, and admirable. Think about things that are excellent and worthy of praise.
—PHILIPPIANS 4:6-8 - NLT

Thou wilt keep him in perfect peace, whose mind is stayed on thee: because he trusteth in thee. Trust ye in the LORD for ever: for in the LORD JEHOVAH is everlasting strength. —ISAIAH 26:3-4 - KJV

For those who are according to the flesh set their minds on the things of the flesh, but those who are according to the Spirit, the things of the Spirit. For the mind set on the flesh is death, but the mind set on the Spirit is life and peace, because the mind set on the flesh is hostile toward God; for it does not subject itself to the law of God, for it is not even able to do so, and those who are in the flesh cannot please God.
—ROMANS 8:5-8

Cast your burden upon the LORD and He will sustain

you... "*My peace I give to you...Do not let your heart be troubled...*
Do not be unbelieving, but believing." —Psalm 55:22; John 14:27; 20:27
Is anyone among you suffering? Then he must pray... "And
lo, I am with you always." — James 5:13; Matthew 28:20

PRAYER

Blessed Savior, thank You for Your promises and provisions of peace for Your followers. As I reflect on Your peace today, I realize how much I have been doubting the truth of it. And my mind has been focused on the physical issues in my life, and desires for fulfillment in things that seem to leave me empty.

Forgive me for not setting my faith upon Your promise of peace, and for relying on my own learned beliefs and perspectives to rule my mind and heart. I long to have a vibrant spiritual relationship with You that can overshadow any benefits from physical pleasures or the worries that tend to dominate. And in Your Presence, extreme peace flows from You and fills my being!

I surrender all and admit that I can't control people, plans, or circumstances, but I *can* yield those things to You, and focus on Your goodness. I know that when I pray and give thanks instead of worrying, You have promised that I can experience unfathomable peace. That's Your kind of peace, Lord, and it's the kind I crave.

By Your Holy Spirit, help me to intentionally replace feelings and thoughts of anxiety and worry. Instead, fill my mind with Your Word and promises, that I stand upon them today in faith! Replace thoughts and images in my mind that would steal precious moments with You. I ask that You bless and guide my mind and heart to remain focused on You, and Help me walk-out these commitments to You and myself each day. Amen

MOMENT OF GRATITUDE: Thank You today for every good gift You've given, every blessing You've sent, all the forgiveness I did not deserve, and, yes, even for every trial You've allowed into my life. You bring good out of every circumstance if I'll only let go and believe You. I am so thankful You called me out of darkness, and are my Friend forever!

17. PRAYER FOR THE FRUIT OF PEACE

PRAYERS FOR PEACE

*B*lessed are the peacemakers, for they shall be called* *sons of God…Great peace have those who love Your law, and nothing causes them to stumble.*
—MATTHEW 5:9; PSALM 119:165 - NKJ

But the wisdom from above is first pure [morally and spiritually undefiled], then peace-loving [courteous, considerate], gentle, reasonable [and willing to listen], full of compassion and good fruits.
It is unwavering, without [self-righteous] hypocrisy [and self-serving guile]. And the seed whose fruit is righteousness (spiritual maturity) is sown in peace by those who make peace [by actively encouraging goodwill between individuals]. —JAMES 3:17-18 - AMP

Rejoice in the Lord always; again I will say, rejoice! Let your gentle spirit be known to all men. The Lord is near. —PHILIPPIANS 4: 4-5

SERENITY PRAYER —Attributed to Francis of Assisi

Lord, make me an instrument of Your peace.
where there is hatred, let me sow love; where there is injury, pardon;
where there is doubt, faith; where there is despair, hope; Where
there is darkness, light; where there is sadness, joy;
O Divine Master, grant that I may not so much seek to be consoled
as to console; Not so much to be understood as to understand;
Not so much to be loved as to love. For it is in giving that we
receive, it is in pardoning that we are pardoned;
And it is in dying of the self that we are born to eternal life.

PRAYER

THIS DAY LORD, HELP ME TO SEEK YOUR WISDOM AND WALK IN A peaceful spirit. Increase my faith, oh Lord, and help me claim Your promise of peace with confidence and assurance. Teach me to be humble and obedient to Your leading so I may continue on Your path of peace, to submit faithfully to Your will, and eternally enter Your peaceful rest from this moment forward.

I ask to remain in a bond of love with You and with my fellow believers, so that I may have the honor of producing Your fruits of goodness for others' sake. Give me wisdom in situations to be a

"peace-maker"—not to instigate any form of unrest, conflict, or agitation. To put out flames of controversy with the principles found in Your Word.

Lord, Help me to love You and Your Word with greater passion and desire, that as I earnestly seek both, the transformation of my mind and heart through Your Holy Spirit will cause me to walk firmly and confidently in Your pathway of peace. Then Your "living waters" of true peace may flow freely into and through me, to others.

MOMENT OF GRATITUDE: Thank You God, that You have gifted us with Your Spirit, the Comforter, Intercessor, Advocate, and Strengthener within, as our continuous Helper and Friend!

PRAYERS OF GRATITUDE

*Prayer should not be regarded as a duty which
must be performed,
but rather as a privilege to be enjoyed,
a rare delight that is always revealing some
new beauty.*

—E.M. Bounds

THANKFUL FOR GRACE

Now thank we all our God
with heart and hands and voices,
who wondrous things has done,
in whom his world rejoices;
who from our mothers' arms
has blessed us on our way
with countless gifts of love,
and still is ours today.
...
All praise and thanks to God
the Father now be given,
the Son and Spirit blest,
who reign in highest heaven
the one eternal God,
whom heaven and earth adore;
for thus it was, is now,
and shall be evermore.

—MARTIN RINKART, 1636

18. GRATITUDE FOR NEW LIFE IN HIS LOVE

PRAYERS of GRATITUDE

*T*o him who loves us and has freed us from our sins by *His* blood, and has made us to be a kingdom and priests to serve his God and Father—to him be glory and power for ever and ever! Amen. —REVELATION 1:5-6 - NIV

Many waters cannot quench love..for love is as strong as death..."Greater love has no one than this: to lay down one's life for one's friends."
—SONGS OF SOLOMON 8:6; JOHN 15:13 - NIV

"He himself bore our sins" in his body on the cross, so that we might die to sins and live for righteousness; "by his wounds you have been healed." —1 PETER 2:24 - NIV (PETER QUOTES ISAIAH 53)

In him we have redemption through his blood, the forgiveness of sins, in accordance with the riches of God's grace...But you were washed, you were sanctified, you were justified in the name of the Lord Jesus Christ and by the Spirit of our God.
—EPHESIANS 1:7; 1 CORINTHIANS 6:11 - NIV

But you are a chosen people, a royal priesthood, a holy nation, God's special possession, that you may declare the praises of him who called you out of darkness into his wonderful light.
—1 PETER 2:9 - NIV

...and in Him you have been made complete, and He is the head over all rule and authority. —COLOSSIANS 2:10

Therefore, I urge you, brothers and sisters, in view of God's mercy, to offer your bodies as a living sacrifice, holy and pleasing to God—this is your true and proper worship. Do not conform to the pattern of this world, but be transformed by the renewing of your mind. Then you will be able to test and approve what God's will is— his good, pleasing and perfect will. —ROMANS 12:1-2 - NIV

PRAYER

Lord Jesus, risen gloriously from the dead, I worship You as my living Savior Who redeemed me to be Your own eternally. I adore You as conqueror of Satan, sin, and death. Joy fills my heart as I worship You, my eternal living Lord; for death cannot hold us in terror, and even the grave cannot keep our dust and ashes. I need not weep despairing tears, for You will raise me and all believers to eternal life.

Oh, my loving Lord, my merciful God, and my gracious King—I bless and honor You with the sacrifice of my own life in service to You. Take full possession of my heart today, I open it up to You, fill it with joy.

Cleanse me from all sinful desires and actions. I give You my lips to bring praises to Your Name. I give my time and talents, for Your divine will and purpose; use them, I pray. Let not the worries of this life rob me of the joys of Your Gospel! Jesus, in Your Name, Amen.

MOMENT OF GRATITUDE: I am grateful that You have rescued me from the dominion of darkness and transferred me into Your marvelous Kingdom of Your beloved Son in whom I have redemption, the forgiveness of sins. And no man, no thing, no power in hell can undo what He did on the cross. (Based on Colossians 1)

19. GRATITUDE FOR JESUS' LOVE & COMPASSION

PRAYERS of GRATITUDE

*T*HE LOVE OF GOD TOWARD US THRU JESUS CHRIST: **But when the goodness and loving kindness of** *God our Savior appeared, he saved us, not because of works done by us in righteousness, but according to his own mercy, by the washing of regeneration and renewal of the Holy Spirit, whom he poured out on us richly through Jesus Christ our Savior, so that being justified by his grace we might become heirs according to the hope of eternal life.* —TITUS 3:4-7 - ESV

But because of his great love for us, God, who is rich in mercy, made us alive with Christ even when we were dead in transgressions—it is by grace you have been saved. And God raised us up with Christ and seated us with him in the heavenly realms in Christ Jesus.
—EPHESIANS 2:4-6 - NIV

Neither height nor depth, nor anything else in all creation, will be able to separate us from the love of God that is in Christ Jesus our Lord.
—ROMANS 8:39 - NIV

JESUS SHOWED US THE FATHER'S LOVE & COMPASSION: *"He who has seen Me has seen the Father."* —JOHN 14:9

He saw a large crowd, and felt compassion for them and healed their sick. —Matthew 14:14

The Spirit of the Lord GOD is upon me, because the LORD has anointed me to bring good news to the afflicted; He has sent me to bind up the brokenhearted, To proclaim liberty to captives and freedom to prisoners... giving them a garland instead of ashes, The oil of gladness instead of mourning, The mantle of praise instead of a spirit of fainting. So they will be called oaks of righteousness, the planting of the LORD, that He may be glorified. —Isaiah 61:1-3

Prayer

Saved by Your grace, Jesus, my Friend, I stand in wonder that You revealed Yourself to me personally. Thank You for loving me and drawing me to Yourself, to become a member of your family!

Jesus, I am also amazed to learn of Your personal actions of love, compassion, gentleness, and tenderhearted care that You displayed during Your time on earth. And how these same actions reveal our Father to me, as He has these same characteristics and feelings toward me as well! I ask that You make these even more real to me, so that I see the reality of Your loving compassion in the deepest depths of my heart and in all my thoughts.

My heart is filled with gratitude! Guide me this day so I remain close to You, my Savior. Help me remain focused on the awareness of Your presence with me every moment! Remove from me careless thoughts and words that do not reflect who I am in You.

In Your grace, I am living in Christ and seated with Him in heavenly love, joy, and peace—this new life with You is truly living! I am renewed by Your Holy Spirit and blessed by the solid hope that nothing can separate me from Your loving arms.

Moment of Gratitude: I am eternally grateful that, in love, You have spread out great blessings upon me! Help me take hold of Your love and fully accept Your adornments of gladness, praise, and strength. May Your beauty rest upon me this day and always.

20. THANKSGIVING FOR REDEMPTION

PRAYERS of GRATITUDE

For God so [greatly] loved and dearly prized the world,
that He [even] gave His [One and] only begotten Son,
so that whoever believes and trusts in Him [as Savior]
shall not perish, but have eternal life.
For God did not send the Son
into the world to judge and condemn the world
[that is, to initiate the final judgment of the world],
but that the world might be saved through Him.
—JOHN 3:16-17 - AMP

Behold! The Lamb of God who takes away the sin of the world!
...Jesus...said, "It is finished!" And bowing His head, He gave up His
spirit. —JOHN 1:29,19:30 - NKJ

By one sacrifice he has made perfect forever those who are
being made holy. —HEBREWS 10:14 - NIV

Bless the LORD, O my soul, and all that is within me,
bless His holy name.
Bless the LORD, O my soul,

and forget none of His benefits;

...

Who redeems your life from the pit,
who crowns you with lovingkindness and compassion;
Who satisfies your years with good things,
So that your youth is renewed like the eagle.

...

The LORD is compassionate and gracious,
Slow to anger and abounding in lovingkindness.
—PSALM 103:1-2,4-5,8

Prayer

G reat and merciful God and Father, I appear before you with gratitude in my heart and praise on my lips. I cannot express my extreme gratefulness for Your gift of eternal life through Jesus, Holy Lamb of God.

Bless me with Your abiding presence this day, Oh Lord. I love You. Oh, my Lord, my God, and my King—Your immense love and compassion give strength to those who dwell near You. Thank You that in this new life I live in You, I am renewed and energized by Your presence and filled with extreme love.

Keep me from veering away from You in thoughts, words, or actions. It is so wonderful to be alive in You, living in the fullness of Your awesome joy and peace, and looking forward to eternity in heaven. Take full possession of my heart today. Cleanse me, keep me, let not the cares and worries of life rob me of the joy of your Gospel!

I extol You for opening up Your hands to supply my needs and Your heart to invite me into relationship with You! Yours be the praise, throughout all eternity, Amen. Hallelujah! Amen.

MOMENT OF GRATITUDE: I Thank You, God, for my real identity in You—for You are my Friend and King. I am valued, loved, and redeemed. I am not what the world says about me, but what You say. Gratitude fills my heart with joy!

PRAYERS FOR JOY

*And though you have not seen Him,
you love Him,
and though you do not see Him now,
but believe in Him,
you greatly rejoice with joy inexpressible
and full of glory,
obtaining as the outcome of your faith
the salvation of your souls.*
—1 Peter 1:8-9

*In Your presence is fullness of joy; In Your
right hand there are pleasures forever.*
—Psalm 16:11

JOY FROM THE PRESENCE OF GOD

The Joy of the Lord is your strength. —Nehemiah 8:10

Joyful, joyful, we adore You,
God of glory, Lord of love;
Hearts unfold like flow'rs before You,
Op'ning to the sun above.
Melt the clouds of sin and sadness;
Drive the dark of doubt away;
Giver of immortal gladness,
Fill us with the light of day!
...
Always giving and forgiving,
Ever blessing, ever blest,
Well-spring of the joy of living,
Ocean-depth of happy rest!
Loving Father, Christ our Brother,
Let Your light upon us shine;
Teach us how to love each other,
Lift us to the joy divine.

—HENRY VAN DYKE, 1907

21. PRAYER FOR HIS JOY IN YOU

PRAYERS FOR JOY

*T*HE CLOSER WE ABIDE IN HIM THE DEEPER OUR JOY:

> *"I am the true vine...Abide in Me and I in you...These things I have spoken unto you, that My joy might remain in you, and that your joy might be full."* —JOHN 15:1,4,11 - KJV

> *"Do not be grieved, for the joy of the LORD is your strength."*
> —NEHEMIAH 8:10

> *When my anxious thoughts multiply within me, Your consolations delight my soul...You have put gladness in my heart, more than when their grain and new wine abound.* —PSALMS 94:19; 4:7

> *You will make known to me the path of life;*
> *In Your presence is fullness of joy;*
> *In Your right hand there are pleasures forever.* —PSALM 16:11

JESUS' LAST PRAYER BEFORE HIS CRUCIFIXION WAS FOR US TO HAVE EXCEEDING JOY:

"I pray for them...I will remain in the world no longer, but they are still in the world...Holy Father, protect them by the power of your name... so that they may be one as we are one...I am coming to you now, but I say these things while I am still in the world, so that they may have the full measure of my joy within them."
—JOHN 17:9,11,13 - NIV

PRAYER

Heavenly Father, Your presence truly fills me with unexplainable joy!

I have seen how abiding in You fills me with great delight! I have also experienced how the unbelief of doubt, worry, and self-sufficiency can steal away Your presence and joy from me. You did not leave, but there are times that I have "walked away" from You. But when I lay down my anxieties and cares in faith, then I no longer put faith in worry or accomplishments, but in You! So I ask with all my heart, show me the great depths of Your life within me. Open my eyes to always see, to always remain in You, so that I may always draw from Your well of joy, in good times and bad.

My Father, as Your child, I am encouraged when thinking how You delight in me. Your Fatherly joy fills my heart with warmth. As my heavenly Father, You smile lovingly and rejoice even over my small steps of faith. When I stumble, learning from my mistakes, Your compassion brings comfort and assurance.

Let me ever be filled with joy that You drew me with bands of kindness, and Your love for me is assured. Help me never stop seeking the treasure of drawing nearer to Your joyful presence. Amen.

MOMENT OF GRATITUDE: I am grateful to be Your little lamb, living in You, and breathing in Your peaceful presence with joyful delight. I extend my deepest gratitude that You made me to have the capacity to feel Your joy, and You have also given it to me as a gift of intimacy with You! Thank You!

22. PRAYER FOR LIFESTYLE OF JOY

PRAYERS FOR JOY

*R**ejoice with those who rejoice.* —Romans 12:15

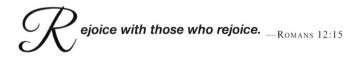

But the fruit of the Spirit is love, joy, peace, patience, kindness,
*goodness, faithfulness, gentleness, self-control; against such things
there is no law. Now those who belong to Christ Jesus have
crucified the flesh with its passions and desires. If we live by the
Spirit, let us also walk by the Spirit.*
—Galatians 5:22-25

You will make known to me the path of life;
*In Your presence is fullness of joy;
In Your right hand there are pleasures forever.* —Psalm 16:11

Always be full of joy in the Lord. I say it again—rejoice! Let
*everyone see that you are considerate in all you do. Remember, the
Lord is coming soon.* —Philippians 4:4-5 -NLT

Blessed are the people who know the joyful sound! They walk,
O LORD, in the light of Your countenance. In Your name they rejoice
all day long, And in Your righteousness they are exalted. For You are
the glory of their strength, And in Your favor our horn is exalted.
—PSALM 89:15-17 - NKJ

PRAYER

JESUS, I AM WALKING IN FREEDOM AND FELLOWSHIP WITH YOUR HOLY Spirit. In kindness and goodness You have drawn me out of a dark land of bondage ruled by fleshly passions that deny Your existence. I give these up willingly to live in Your joy. My life hidden in You and Your inexpressible joy far exceed any benefit I may have received from anything the world has to offer.

Please help me to always maintain a positive, considerate attitude that rejoices with others. Let Your joy flow through me so it may be seen by others! I would like to be a witness for You in everything I do—guide me Lord, and I will obey and submit to Your guidance.

Heavenly Father, if I walk every day in the light of Your countenance, all my worries and concerns will fade away in Your glory! Help me to walk today in this way; with my eyes focused on You, it will be impossible for me to stumble!

Help me to ever come closer to You, to be increasingly aware of Your presence with me. Kindle in me a greater love that I may joyfully serve You and those around me. In Jesus' Name, Amen.

MOMENT OF GRATITUDE: Thank You for the extreme joy and peace we can only find in You alone. My gratitude overflows in a delightful melody that fills my heart. I celebrate my life in You, and praise You for all these wonderful blessings.

23. PRAYER TO KNOW JOY OF THE GOSPEL

PRAYERS FOR JOY

*J*ESUS: *...through him we have obtained access by faith into this grace in which we stand, and we rejoice in the hope of the glory of God.* —ROMANS 5:2 - ESV

Blessed be the God and Father of our Lord Jesus Christ, who *according to His great mercy has caused us to be born again to a living hope through the resurrection of Jesus Christ from the dead, to obtain an inheritance which is imperishable and undefiled and will not fade away, reserved in heaven for you...and though you have not seen Him, you love Him, and though you do not see Him now, but believe in Him, you greatly rejoice with joy inexpressible_and full of glory, obtaining as the outcome of your faith the salvation of your souls.* —1 PETER 1:3-4-9

In Him we have redemption through His blood, the *forgiveness of sins, according to the riches of His grace...rejoicing in hope, patient in tribulation, continuing steadfastly in prayer.*

—EPHESIANS 1:7; ROMANS 12:12 - NKJ

...The faith and love that spring from the hope stored up for *you in heaven and about which you have already heard in the true message of the gospel that has come to you. In the same way, the gospel is bearing fruit and growing throughout the whole world—just*

as it has been doing among you since the day you heard it and truly understood God's grace. —Colossians 1:5-6 - NIV

LET US REJOICE LOOKING FORWARD TO HIS 2ND COMING:
Let us rejoice and be glad and give the glory to Him, for the marriage of the Lamb has come and His bride has made herself ready. —Revelation 19:7

For who is our hope, or joy, or crown of exultation? Is it not *even you in the presence of our Lord Jesus Christ at His coming?* [1]
Thessalonians 2:19

Prayer

By faith, I rejoice because Your Word declares the goodness of eternal life upon us! I am free to sing in jubilance, dancing in my heart before my loving King! No man, no thing, no power in hell can undo what You did on the cross. I joyously praise You that I am saved from the sting of death through Your blood, Holy Lamb of God; I will never be separated from Your gracious loving presence.

Lord, sometimes I feel weak. When I leave You behind and walk ahead, taking control of issues in my life apart from You, worry and doubt creep in. Then my joy begins to slip away. Forgive me for trying to solve my problems without You. Today, help me stand firmly upon Your grace in faith. Then I will find hope to rejoice in Your glorious promises. I truly desire to live by faith in You for everything in my life. My accomplishments or goals are nothing without You!

Give me boldness to share Your testimony of salvation with others today, with a passion that desires no one to perish and spend eternity separated from You.

Help me to walk out these days on earth with the joyful purpose of spreading the good news of Your amazing offer of grace and eternal life to those in my life! Jesus, I am excited about seeing You at the wedding feast You are preparing for us!

MOMENT OF GRATITUDE: I will praise You with great joy and thanksgiving, that You have made a way for me to spend eternal life with You through Jesus shed blood. He is my living hope, resurrected from the dead, my eternal life! I praise Your Holy Name!

24. PRAYER FOR THE JOY OF PRAISE & THANKSGIVING

PRAYERS FOR JOY

*S**hout joyfully to the LORD, all the earth. Serve the LORD** with gladness; Come before Him with joyful singing. Know that the LORD Himself is God; It is He who has made us, and not we ourselves; We are His people and the sheep of His pasture.*

__Enter His gates with thanksgiving, and His courts with__ praise. Give thanks to Him, bless His name. For the LORD is good; His lovingkindness is everlasting and His faithfulness to all generations. —PSALM 100

Rejoice in the LORD,
O you righteous!
For praise from the upright is beautiful.
—PSALM 33:1 - NKJ

Make a joyful noise to the LORD, all the earth;
break forth into joyous song and sing praises! Sing praises to the LORD with the lyre, with the lyre and the sound of melody! With trumpets and the sound of the horn make a joyful noise before the King, the LORD! —PSALM 98:4-6 - ESV

I have seen you in the sanctuary and beheld your power *and your glory. Because your love is better than life,*

my lips will glorify you. I will praise you as long as I live,
and in your name I will lift up my hands.
I will be fully satisfied as with the richest of foods;
with singing lips my mouth will praise you. —PSALM 63:2-5 - NIV

PRAYER

Thank You for King David's timeless examples in the Psalms of how to walk in faith, hope and joy! In faith today I claim "Your love is better than life" Oh Lord You bless me simply by allowing me to sense Your joy. Because You feed me in the richness of Your Word and Spirit, I sing praise in my heart and am delighted by communion with Your Spirit, my heavenly Father.

The revelation of You as King and Lord of my life has brought delight and singing to my heart. When I stray, my joy decreases. Today, with the help of Your Holy Spirit, I will take a fresh audit of my heart and intentions to see if You reign supremely—whether I allow Your rule over my words, thoughts, and actions. Help me focus and seek understanding of *how* to truly praise You with a pure heart.

Help me put on that beautiful garment of thanksgiving! And give me wisdom to worship You in spirit and in truth.

MOMENT OF GRATITUDE:
All Your works with joy surround You,
Earth and heav'n reflect Your rays,
Stars and angels sing around You,
Center of unbroken praise;
Field and forest, vale and mountain,
Flow'ry meadow, flashing sea,
Chanting bird and flowing fountain
Praising You eternally!

—HENRY VAN DYKE, 1907

PRAYER FOR SALVATION

The most amazing things about the journey of salvation begin with the miracle of hearing the call of God! That our eyes were opened to see clearly our need for an intimate friendship with our Father and for His new life. Then the realization that Jesus made the only way possible for that to happen—He paid our debt to God by shedding His perfect blood on our behalf.

"For God so loved the world, that He gave His only begotten Son, that whoever believes in Him shall not perish, but have eternal life."

— JESUS CHRIST, JOHN 3:16

Blest is the man, forever blest,
Whose guilt is pardoned by his God,
Whose sins with sorrow are confessed
And covered with his Savior's blood.

Blest is the man to whom the Lord
Imputes not his iniquities;
He pleads no merit of reward
And not on works but grace relies.

From guile his heart and lips are free;
His humble joy, his holy fear,
With deep repentance well agree
And join to prove his faith sincere.

How glorious is that righteousness
That hides and cancels all his sins,
While bright the evidence of grace
Thro' all his life appears and shines!

—ISAAC WATTS 1719
(INSPIRED BY PSALM 32)

25. PRAYER FOR SALVATION

YHWH *Maccaddeshcem*: "I am the LORD who sanctifies you."

— EXODUS 31:13

YHWH *Tsidkenu*: The LORD our righteousness.

— JEREMIAH 23:6

*J*ESUS SANCTIFIES US, HE IS OUR RIGHTEOUSNESS. *But through His own blood, He entered the holy place once for all, having obtained eternal redemption. ...For this reason He is the mediator of a new covenant, so that, since a death has taken place for the redemption of the transgressions that were committed under the first covenant, those who have been called may receive the promise of the eternal inheritance.* —Hebrews 9:12,15

Salvation Prayer

You can have a restored relationship with God and enter into eternal life today by asking Jesus to become your Savior. Pray a prayer like the one below or use your own words:

Jesus, I believe that You are the son of God, and You died and rose again so that I might be accepted as His child. I know that I'm a sinner and my actions against God are very real, both physical and spiritual.

I ask You to wash me clean and forgive me, help me turn from my sins and show me how to follow You daily. Please come into my heart and be the Lord of my life from today forward.

Since, I receive Your forgiveness today and have now received a new spiritual life from you, I ask you to show me how to live this new life, as pleasing to You. Guide me as I seek to know You as my Friend and Lord—help me find a deep abiding relationship with You.

Thank You, Lord, I now have hope and peace that when I leave this life on earth, I will go on living in Your glorious eternal life! Amen.

MOMENT OF GRATITUDE: Lord Jesus, risen gloriously from the dead, I worship You as my living Savior, who redeemed me to be Your own eternally; and I adore You as conqueror of Satan, sin, and death. Joy fills my heart as I worship You, the eternal, living Lord; You will raise me and all believers to eternal life in that glorious day.

Take full possession of my heart today. Let not the cares and worries of life rob me of the joy of Your Gospel! Yours be the praise, throughout all eternity. Amen. Hallelujah! Amen.

WE ARE THEN SANCTIFIED, OUR RIGHTEOUSNESS IS HIM

The path to redemption begins not with the decision to live a better life or to stop doing something "wrong", but with the realization that we cannot correct our sinful nature. To find favor with the Lord, we must recognize that we cannot make ourselves good enough. Instead, we need to depend completely upon the sacrifice Jesus made on our behalf, and our relationship with Him.

Behold! The Lamb of God who takes away the sin of the world!...He said, "It is finished!" And bowing His head, He gave up His spirit. —JOHN 1:29;19:30 - NKJ

By one sacrifice he has made perfect forever those who are being made holy...Having canceled the charge of our legal indebtedness, which stood against us and condemned us; he has taken it away, nailing it to the cross.
—HEBREWS 10:14; COLOSSIANS 2:14 - NIV

And by that will, we have been made holy through the sacrifice of the body of Jesus Christ once for all. —But when this priest had offered for all time one sacrifice for sins, he sat down at the right hand of God, and since that time he waits for his enemies to be made his footstool.
—HEBREWS 10:10,12-13 - NIV

∾

THIS NEW LIFE IN CHRIST IS OURS AT THE MOMENT WE BELIEVE AND MAKE HIM LORD OF OUR LIVES

REDEEMED FROM DEATH UNTO NEW & ETERNAL LIFE:

This is eternal life, that they may know You, the only true God, and Jesus Christ whom You have sent. —JOHN 17:3

Since the children have flesh and blood, he too shared in their humanity so that by his death he might break the power of him who holds the power of death—that is, the devil...But now in Christ Jesus you who once were far away have been brought near by the blood of Christ. For he himself is our peace. —Hebrews 2:14; Ephesians 2:13-14 - NIV

For this is how God loved the world: He gave his one and only Son, so that everyone who believes in him will not perish but have eternal life. God sent his Son into the world not to judge the world, but to save the world through him. —John 3:16-17 - NLT

In this was manifested the love of God toward us, because that God sent his only begotten Son into the world, that we might live through him. Herein is love, not that we loved God, but that he loved us, and sent his Son to be the propitiation for our sins. —1 John 4:9-10 - KJV

This new life is a spiritual re-birth
*Jesus answered and said to him,
"Truly, truly, I say to you, unless one is born again he cannot see the kingdom of God."* —John 3:3

Why Does God Require Blood for the Redemption of our Soul?

"Greater love has no man than this, that a man lay down his life for his friends..." For the life of the flesh is in the blood: and I have given it to you upon the altar to make atonement for your souls; for it is the blood that maketh an atonement for the soul. —John 15:13; Leviticus 17:11- KJV

For it was the Father's good pleasure for all the fullness to dwell in Him, and through Him to reconcile all things to Himself, having made peace through the blood of His cross; through Him... —Colossians 1:19-20

WHY DID JESUS DO THAT FOR US?

HE LOVES ALL PEOPLE AND DESIRES TO HAVE A PERSONAL RELATIONSHIP WITH YOU!

"At that time," declares the Lord, "I will be the God of all the families of Israel, and they will be my people"..."This is the covenant I will make with the people of Israel after that time," declares the Lord. "I will put my law in their minds and write it on their hearts. I will be their God, and they will be my people." —JEREMIAH 31:1,33 - NIV

But when the goodness and loving kindness of God our Savior appeared, he saved us, not because of works done by us in righteousness, but according to his own mercy, by the washing of regeneration and renewal of the Holy Spirit, whom he poured out on us richly through Jesus Christ our Savior, so that being justified by his grace we might become heirs according to the hope of eternal life. —TITUS 3:4-7 - ESV

And so we know and rely on the love God has for us. God is love. Whoever lives in love lives in God, and God in them. —1 JOHN 4:16 - NIV

"Abide in Me, and I in you. As the branch cannot bear fruit of itself unless it abides in the vine, so neither can you unless you abide in Me. I am the vine, you are the branches; he who abides in Me and I in him, he bears much fruit; for apart from Me you can do nothing." —JOHN 15:4-5

How precious also are Your thoughts to me, O God! How great is the sum of them! If I should count them, they would be more in number than the sand; When I awake, I am still with You. —PSALM 139:17-18 - NKJ

The LORD's lovingkindnesses indeed never cease, For His compassions never fail. They are new every morning; —LAMENTATIONS 3:22-23

I sat down under his shadow with great delight, and his fruit was sweet to my taste. He brought me to the banqueting house, and his banner over me was love. —SONG OF SOLOMON 2:3-4 - KJV

THE LORD'S PRAYER

MATTHEW 6:9-13

THE LORD'S PRAYER

Our Father who is in heaven,
Hallowed be Your name.

Your kingdom come.
Your will be done,
On earth as it is in heaven.

Give us this day our daily bread.

And forgive us our debts, as we also have forgiven our debtors.

And do not lead us into temptation, but deliver us from evil.
[For Yours is the kingdom and the power and the glory forever.
Amen.]

Our Father, Thou in heav'n above,
Who biddest us to dwell in love,
As brethren of one family,
And cry for all we need to Thee;
Teach us to mean the words we say,
And from the inmost heart to pray.

All hallowed be Thy name, O Lord!
O let us firmly keep Thy Word,
And lead, according to Thy name,
A holy life, untouched by blame;
Let no false teachings do us hurt;
All poor deluded souls convert.

Thy kingdom come! Thine let it be
In time and in eternity!
O let Thy Holy Spirit dwell
With us, to rule and guide us well;
From Satan's mighty pow'r and rage
Preserve Thy Church from age to age.

Thy will be done on earth, O Lord,
As where in heav'n Thou art adored!
Patience in time of grief bestow,
Obedience true in weal and woe;
Our sinful flesh and blood control
That thwart Thy will within the soul.

Give us this day our daily bread,
Let us be duly clothed and fed;
And keep Thou from our homes afar
Famine and pestilence and war,
That we may live in godly peace

Unvexed by cares and avarice.

Forgive our sins, that they no more
May grieve and haunt us as before,
As we forgive their trespasses
Who unto us have done amiss;
Thus let us dwell in charity
And serve each other willingly.

Into temptation lead us not.
And when the foe doth war and plot
Against our souls on ev'ry hand,
Then armed with faith, O may we stand
Against him as a valiant host
Through comfort of the Holy Ghost.

Deliv'rance from all evil give,
And yet in evil days we live.
Redeem us from eternal death,
And, when we yield our dying breath,
Console us, grant us calm release,
And take our souls to Thee in peace.

Amen! That is, so shall it be!
Strengthen our faith and trust in Thee
That we may doubt not, but believe
That what we ask we shall receive.
Thus in Thy name and at Thy word
We say:"Amen. Now hear us, Lord."

—**MARTIN LUTHER, 1539**
(INSPIRED BY MATTHEW 6:9-13)

26. OUR FATHER WHO IS IN HEAVEN

*O*ur *Father who is in heaven, Hallowed be Your name.* —MATTHEW 6:9

"I will be a father to you, And you shall be sons and daughters to Me," Says the Lord Almighty. —2 CORINTHIANS 6:18
Draw near to God and He will draw near to you. —JAMES 4:8
"Just as the Father has loved Me, I have also loved you; abide in my love." —JOHN 15:9
For you are all children of God through faith in Christ Jesus...
And because we are his children, God has sent the Spirit of his Son into our hearts, prompting us to call out, "Abba, Father."
—GALATIANS 3:26; 4:6 - NLT (Also see Romans 8:15)

And so, dear brothers and sisters, we can boldly enter heaven's Most Holy Place because of the blood of Jesus...let us go right into the presence of God with sincere hearts fully trusting him. For our guilty consciences have been sprinkled with Christ's blood to make us clean, and our bodies have been washed with pure water.
—HEBREWS 10:19,22 - NLT

"HOLY, HOLY, HOLY is THE LORD, THE GOD ALMIGHTY..."
At the name of Jesus EVERY KNEE WILL BOW, of those who are in heaven and on earth and under the earth...

Praise the LORD! For it is good to sing praises to our God; For it is pleasant and praise is becoming.
—REVELATION 4:8; PHILIPPIANS 2:10; PSALM 147:1

Worship the LORD in the Beauty of Holiness!
—1 CHRONICLES 16:29 - NKJ

PRAYER

Our Father in heaven, hallowed be Your name. Today I declare in faith that You are my Father and Your name is Holy. As Your child, I thank You for making a way for me to come close to You at any time I wish...whether I need something or not. Sometimes I just like to sit on Your lap and be near You.

By the blood of Jesus, I have confidence to enter into Your Holy Place. Through Him I have a peaceful assurance to come near You with faith in my heart, and a clean conscience because He took away all the debt/guilt I felt from past behaviors I know weren't right.

My loving Father, I now come before You in purity of heart, longing to make You happy as You have also made me. I know I will not be perfect, but my heart's desire is to walk and abide in You, in love. You understand my weaknesses, and when I fail, You help me get back up. And for that I love You even more!

Being with You is so incredible, I just want to worship and praise You, and when I do I feel beautiful! Praising and thanking You renews my own spirit and that makes sense since You do inhabit the praises of Your people!*

Joy fills me as I praise Your Holy name with a wonderful song in my heart all the day—it is like perfume to my heart, and salvation to my soul. Let me honor You today as I go about my daily schedule in my thoughts, my words, and my actions. To You be all the glory, Amen.

MOMENT OF GRATITUDE: I am grateful that You loved me enough to bring me into Your family. You are my Father! Thank You that You are always there for me at any time, waiting with open arms.

* (Psalm 22:3)

27. YOUR KINGDOM COME

*Y*our kingdom come.
—Matthew 6:10 a

The LORD has established His throne in the heavens, And His sovereignty rules over all...Your kingdom is an everlasting kingdom, and Your dominion endures throughout all generations. —Psalms 103:19;145:13

"But this is the new covenant I will make with the people of Israel after those days," says the LORD. "I will put my instructions deep within them, and I will write them on their hearts. I will be their God, and they will be my people." —Jeremiah 31:33 - NLT

Jesus established God's Spiritual Kingdom:
He answered them and said, "The kingdom of God does not come with observation; nor will they say, 'See here!' or 'See there!' For indeed, the kingdom of God is within you."
—Luke 17:20-21 - NKJ

All who declare that Jesus is the Son of God have God living in them, and they live in God. —1 John 4:15 - NLT
But we are citizens of heaven, where the Lord Jesus Christ lives. And we are eagerly waiting for him to return as our Savior.
— Philippians 3:20 - NLT

JESUS WILL ESTABLISH THE FULLNESS OF GOD'S KINGDOM, FROM TIME THROUGHOUT ETERNITY:

So you also must be ready, because the Son of Man will come at an hour when you do not expect him. —MATTHEW 24:44 - NIV

In the time of those kings, the God of heaven will set up a kingdom that will never be destroyed, nor will it be left to another people. It will crush all those kingdoms and bring them to an end, but it will itself endure forever. —DANIEL 2:44 - NIV

The kingdoms of this world have become the kingdoms of our Lord and of His Christ, and He shall reign forever and ever!...and His name is called The Word of God...And He has on His robe and on His thigh a name written: KING OF KINGS AND LORD OF LORDS. —REVELATION 11:15;19:13,16 - NKJ

PRAYER

My Lord, God, and King, let Your kingdom come into my heart and life today. I am humbled before You as I ponder Your kingdom. You are royalty, and as Your child I also share that same dignity and so I feel greatly honored and blessed.

My desire is that You rule and reign in my mind and heart. I pray that by Your Spirit within me, I walk worthy of this position I have in You, that my character and conduct reflect my Holy King in every way.

Help me to always carry a sense of awareness of You and Your kingdom as I go about my daily tasks and responsibilities. That Your agenda, will, and presence remain my true priorities as I live in the visible world around me.

I ask now, as Moses once cried out to You, please do not send me from here unless Your presence goes with me, how else will those around me know that I am a person in Your kingdom?* I know You will be with me today and always! I love You my King.

MOMENT OF GRATITUDE: I praise and thank You for calling me into Your kingdom of light and love, to be with You forever!

*(Based on Exodus 33:15)

28. YOUR WILL BE DONE

Your will be done, on earth as it is in heaven.
—Matthew 6:10 b

It is not the will of your Father who is in heaven that one of these little ones should perish. —Matthew 18:14 - NKJ

Be very careful, then, how you live—not as unwise but as wise, making the most of every opportunity, because the days are evil. Therefore do not be foolish, but understand what the Lord's will is…It is God's will that you should be sanctified.
—Ephesians 5:15-17; 1 Thessalonians 4:3 - NIV

Therefore, since Christ suffered in his body, arm yourselves also with the same attitude…As a result, they do not live the rest of their earthly lives for evil human desires, but rather for the will of God. —1 Peter 4:1-2 - NIV

I HAVE FOUND DAVID the son of Jesse, A MAN AFTER MY HEART, who will do all My will. —Acts 13:22

Jesus our example, "Not my will, but Yours be done":
And He went a little beyond them, and fell on His face and prayed, saying, "My Father, if it is possible, let this cup pass from Me; yet not as I will, but as You will." —Matthew 26:39
Jesus said to them, "My food is to do the will of Him who sent

Me and to accomplish His work...I speak these things as the Father taught Me. And He who sent Me is with Me; He has not left Me alone, for I always do the things that are pleasing to Him."
—John 4:34; 8:28-29

And He said to them, "Why did you seek Me? Did you not know *that I must be about My Father's business?"* —Luke 2:49 - NKJ

Prayer

Heavenly Father, may all Your will be done in my life today. May all aspects of my life, from the foundation of my mind and heart to my home, my business, and all I do or say, honor Your name as an extension of Your life within me.

I especially pray for wisdom that would lead me in Your path of right-living. If I need to make changes to simplify or eliminate things that keep me from spending time with You in Your Word or from walking in Your will, please, I humbly pray, show them to me one by one. Help me follow Your will for every one of these "things" standing in the way, or for behaviors and attitudes.

Give me the heart of David—one that deeply desires to "do *all* Your will." Not just sometimes, but every moment, looking to You for guidance and then obeying it. As Jesus is our example, let me follow in His footsteps to say continually, *"not as I will, but as You will"* in every corner of my life and soul.

Help my mind and heart to become progressively pure in You, that I may also say as Jesus once did, *"My food is to do the will of Him who sent Me and to accomplish His work...I always do the things that are pleasing to Him."* It is true Jesus was perfect and I will make mistakes, but while my mind and heart wholly seek to obey, and my desires shift away from self-fulfillment, then I know I am in the right spiritual position to do the very best possible to fulfill Your will, with the help of Your Holy Spirit!

MOMENT OF GRATITUDE: Thank You for this exciting life, to have the privilege to honor You by seeking and fulfilling Your will!

29. GIVE US THIS DAY OUR DAILY BREAD

*G*ive us this day our daily bread.
—Matthew 6:11

And my God will supply all your needs according to His riches in glory in Christ Jesus. —Philippians 4:19

Man does not live by bread alone, but man lives by everything that proceeds out of the mouth of the LORD.
—Deuteronomy 8:3

"Do not worry then, saying, 'What will we eat?' or 'What will we drink?' or 'What will we wear for clothing?'...for your heavenly Father knows that you need all these things. But seek first His kingdom and His righteousness, and all these things will be added to you. So do not worry about tomorrow; for tomorrow will care for itself. Each day has enough trouble of its own." —Matthew 6:31-34

"I am the living bread that came down from heaven. Whoever eats this bread will live forever. This bread is my flesh, which I will give for the life of the world." —John 6:51 - NIV

Taste and see that the Lord is good. —Psalm 34:8

Does not the ear test words as the tongue tastes food?...I

meditate on your precepts and consider your ways. I delight in your decrees; I will not neglect your word.
—Job 12:11; Psalm 119:15-16 - NIV

***Like newborn babies, you must crave pure spiritual milk so** that you will grow into a full experience of salvation. Cry out for this nourishment, now that you have had a taste of the Lord's kindness.*
—1 Peter 2:2-3 - NLT

***Blessed are those who hunger and thirst for righteousness,** for they shall be satisfied.* —Matthew 5:6

Prayer

My Father, Thank You for caring and feeding me as a loving Shepherd! Because Your Word teaches us that we can trust You to accommodate our basic physical necessities, in faith I will take hold of this promise and believe this is true for me. Please remove thoughts of worry or anxiety about provision. And provide wisdom to help me make right choices about spending money.

Father, I pray for Your guidance today to let my heart "consume" only that which comes from You. I know You created my heart with a desire for joy, peace, and contentment; forgive me for spending time and money on things that only cause me to internalize violence or impurity. As the world darkens, most media / TV programming is full of things that grieve Your Spirit. Instead, Help me choose Your food to edify and satisfy my heart's needs and desires.

Heavenly Father, I sense my hunger and thirst for righteousness has been growing. As I sense Your presence with me, it grows even stronger. Help me to be satisfied on Your pure Word and Holy Spirit, since You have provided both for our spiritual growth and joy.

Moment of Gratitude: Thank You, Father, for Your loving provisions, and that I have tasted Your kindness in my spirit. I now long to always be with You. Thank You for keeping me fed, warm, and clothed. But I am most grateful for the food of Your Word. Protect my mind & heart as I ponder it. I rejoice under Your loving arms.

30. FORGIVE US OUR DEBTS...

*A*nd forgive us our debts, as we also have forgiven our debtors. —Matthew 6:12

When you were dead in your transgressions and the uncircumcision of your flesh, He made you alive together with Him, having forgiven us all our transgressions, having canceled out the certificate of debt consisting of decrees against us, which was hostile to us; and He has taken it out of the way, having nailed it to the cross. —Colossians 2:13-14

He has removed our sins as far from us as the east is from the west. —Psalms 103:12 - NLT

If we confess our sins, he is faithful and just and will forgive us our sins and purify us from all unrighteousness. —1 John 1:9 - NIV

"He himself bore our sins" in his body on the cross, so that we might die to sins and live for righteousness; "by his wounds you have been healed." —1 Peter 2:24 - NIV

Be kind and compassionate to one another, forgiving each other, just as in Christ God forgave you. —Ephesians 4:32 - NIV

In him we have redemption through his blood, the

forgiveness of sins, in accordance with the riches of God's grace.
—Ephesians 1:7 - NIV

But you were washed, you were sanctified, you were justified *in the name of the Lord Jesus Christ and by the Spirit of our God.* —1 Corinthians 6:11 - NIV

For if you forgive other people when they sin against you, *your heavenly Father will also forgive you. But if you do not forgive others their sins, your Father will not forgive your sins.*
—Matthew 6:14-15 - NIV

Then Peter came to Jesus and asked, "Lord, how many times *shall I forgive my brother or sister who sins against me? Up to seven times?" Jesus answered, "I tell you, not seven times, but seventy-seven times."* —Matthew 18:21-22 - NIV

Prayer

O Lord, my merciful Father, I come to You in humble repentance and confess to You the many transgressions of which I am guilty. My sins against you, Father, have been numerous and grievous. But because of Your great love and mercy, it's with confidence I can and do ask for forgiveness. Forgive my iniquities and shortcomings for the sake of Jesus' suffering and death. Let His obedience cover my disobedience, let His righteousness atone for my unrighteousness.

Great God and Helper, You offer me the forgiveness of my sins; with all my heart I thank You for this boundless mercy! Grant that I may accept this divine gift in sincere faith.

You, Heavenly Father, have loved me fully and completely, and have forgiven me, and because a child is like their father, I choose to be like You by forgiving those who have sinned against me. I admit that sometimes it seems impossible for me, but I look to Your Holy Spirit for wisdom and clarity to see what next steps I should take in obedience. I long to grow strong as Your child and submit to the principles You reveal in Your Word.

Moment of Gratitude: I am filled with Your Spirit and am so delighted to feel clean from guilt! Thank You for Jesus' sacrifice that brings eternal life freely to all who accept it!

31. AND DO NOT LEAD US INTO TEMPTATION

And do not lead us into temptation, but deliver us from evil. —Matthew 6:13 a

No temptation has overtaken you but such as is common to man; and God is faithful, who will not allow you to be tempted beyond what you are able, but with the temptation will provide the way of escape also, so that you will be able to endure it.
—1 Corinthians 10:13

When tempted, no one should say, "God is tempting me." For God cannot be tempted by evil, nor does he tempt anyone; but each person is tempted when they are dragged away by their own evil desire and enticed. —James 1:13-14 - NIV

"Therefore, COME OUT FROM THEIR MIDST AND BE SEPARATE," says the Lord. "AND DO NOT TOUCH WHAT IS UNCLEAN; And I will welcome you." —2 Corinthians 6:17

Flee immorality...But I say, walk by the Spirit, and you will not

carry out the desire of the flesh. For the flesh sets its desire against the Spirit... —1 CORINTHIANS 6:18; GALATIANS 5:16-17

He who dwells in the shelter of the Most High will abide in the shadow of the Almighty. *I will say to the Lord, "My refuge and my fortress, My God, in whom I trust!"...*
For He will give His angels charge concerning you, to guard you *in all your ways. They will bear you up in their hands, that you do not strike your foot against a stone...*
Because he has loved Me, therefore I will deliver him; I will set *him securely on high, because he has known My name. He will call upon Me, and I will answer him. I will be with him in trouble; I will rescue him and honor him.* —PSALM 91:1-2,11–12,14-15

PRAYER

Lord Jesus, You have redeemed me by Your blood and called me Your own, a fellow citizen with the saints, a member of Your household. You know all things, and You know I love You.

Help me lay aside desires to walk in the ways of the world, those that cause me to step away from You. I know that You tempt no one, and that I am tempted by my own selfish longings that distract me from You.

Please, O Lord, protect me from my impure thoughts that seek fulfillment apart from You. Turn my eyes firmly in Your direction. I know that in my flesh there is no good thing, and those things I long to do, I don't do—and the things I do not want to do, I do. Please help me to walk by the spirit, and not my flesh. (Romans 6; 8:1-26)

Help me flee into Your arms always! Sanctify and cleanse me wholly, purge every evil desire and thought out of my heart and mind. Fill me with a pure and perfect love for You, that I may do Your will. Protect me from every evil that would come my way to cause hurt or pain—that Your angels would take charge over me to keep me safe! MOMENT OF GRATITUDE: Thank You for showing me how to find joy and happiness in Your Spirit that far exceeds any benefit from sins of lust or personal self-fulfillment.

32. FOR YOURS IS THE KINGDOM AND THE POWER AND THE GLORY FOREVER.

or Yours is the kingdom and the power and the glory forever. Amen. —Matthew 6:13 b

The LORD reigns, He is clothed with majesty;
The LORD has clothed and girded Himself with strength;
Indeed, the world is firmly established, it will not be moved.
Your throne is established from of old;
You are from everlasting. —Psalm 93:1-2

For the LORD Most High is awesome. He is the great King of *all the earth...the LORD God of Heaven's Armies, the LORD is his name!...Who is the King of glory? The LORD of Heaven's Armies— he is the King of glory.* —Psalm 47:2; Hosea 12:5; Psalm 24:10 - NLT

"I am the Alpha and the Omega," says the Lord God, "who is *and who was and who is to come, the Almighty."...And on His robe and on His thigh He has a name written, "KING OF KINGS, AND LORD OF LORDS."* —Revelation 1:8;19:16

Therefore God exalted Him to the highest place and gave *Him the name that is above every name, that at the name of Jesus*

every knee should bow...every tongue acknowledge that Jesus Christ is Lord, to the glory of God the Father. —PHILIPPIANS 2:9-11 - NIV

To him who loves us and has freed us from our sins by His *blood, and has made us to be a kingdom and priests to serve his God and Father—to him be glory and power for ever and ever! Amen.* —REVELATION 1:5-6 - NIV

PRAY THE PRAYER OF DAVID

"Yours, O LORD, is the greatness and the power and the glory and the victory and the majesty, indeed everything that is in the heavens and the earth; Yours is the dominion, O LORD, and You exalt Yourself as head over all. Both riches and honor come from You, and You rule over all, and in Your hand is power and might; and it lies in Your hand to make great and to strengthen everyone.

Now therefore, our God, we thank You, and praise Your glorious name. But who am I and who are my people that we should be able to offer as generously as this? For all things come from You, and from Your hand we have given You."
—1 CHRONICLES 29:11-14

PRAYER

Father, thank You for opening my eyes to see the truth of this great mystery! Lord, my eyes are fixed on You as a young child! With faith of a child, my hope is directed toward living as part of your family in Your Kingdom. In purity of mind I accept it now, and look toward "what I will be..." in that glorious day of Your Revelation.

My hope in Your salvation from eternal death to wonderful life in You is strong, grounded in Your love.

MOMENT OF GRATITUDE: I express my heart-filled thanksgiving to You! I am released from darkness that once ruled my life, to live in Your serenity and peace. Energized by Your Holy Spirit, I worship and praise You, My Lord and King! To You be all the glory, the honor, the praise, throughout all eternity! Hallelujah! Amen.

PRAYERS IN SCRIPTURE

Rejoice always; pray without ceasing; in everything give thanks; for this is God's will for you in Christ Jesus. Do not quench the Spirit.

—1 Thessalonians 5:16-19

This is the confidence which we have before Him, that, if we ask anything according to His will, He hears us. And if we know that He hears us in whatever we ask, we know that we have the requests which we have asked from Him.

—1 John 5:14-15

GOD'S WORD—OUR LIGHT

LAMP of our feet, whereby we trace - Our path when wont to stray,
Stream from the fount of heavenly grace,
- Brook by the traveller's way;

Bread of our souls, whereon we feed, - True manna from on high,
Our guide and chart, wherein we read
- Of realms beyond the sky;

Pillar of fire through watches dark, - And radiant cloud by day,
When waves would whelm our tossing bark,
- Our anchor and our stay;

Word of the ever-living God, - Will of his glorious Son,
Without thee how could earth be trod,
-Or Heaven itself be won?

Lord, grant that we aright may learn - The wisdom it imparts,
And to its heavenly teaching turn - With simple, childlike hearts.

—BERNARD BARTON, 1826

33. PRAYER FOR SPIRITUAL GROWTH—COLOSSIANS

PRAYER FOR SPIRITUAL GROWTH IN SCRIPTURE:

PRAYER BASED ON COLOSSIANS 1:9-14

Heavenly Father, I ask that You fill me with the knowledge of Your will in all spiritual wisdom and understanding, so that I will walk in a manner worthy of You, to please You in all respects, bearing fruit in every good work and increasing in the knowledge of You; please strengthen me in all power, according to Your glorious might, for the attaining of all steadfastness and patience; joyously giving thanks to You, my Father, for qualifying me to share in the inheritance of the saints in Light. For You rescued me from the domain of darkness, and transferred me into the kingdom of Your beloved Son, in whom I have redemption, the forgiveness of sins.

Moment of Gratitude:

(Based on Colossians 1:15-22)

Also joyously giving thanks and praise to You, my beloved Savior Jesus. You are the image of the invisible God, the firstborn of all creation. For by You all things were created, both in the heavens and on earth, visible and invisible, whether thrones or dominions or rulers or authorities—all things have been created through You and for You.

You are before all things, and in You all things hold together.

For You are also head of the body, the church; and You are the beginning, the firstborn from the dead, and I am comforted to know that You Yourself will come to have first place in everything.

For it was Our Father's good pleasure for all the fullness to dwell in You, and through You to reconcile all things to Himself, having made peace through Your blood of the cross; through Him…whether things on earth or things in heaven.

And I am forever grateful that, although I was formerly alienated and hostile in mind, engaged in evil deeds, yet You have now reconciled me by Your fleshly body through death, in order to present me before our Father holy and blameless and beyond reproach.

34. DESPERATE PRAYER FOR HELP—JEHOSHAPHAT'S PRAYER

PRAYER FOR FAITH, COURAGE, & DELIVERANCE
IN TIMES OF TROUBLE

JEHOSHAPHAT'S POWER PRAYER IN 2 CHRONICLES 20:5-25;
LESSONS LEARNED (Pray Through Your Trial using these steps):

hen Jehoshaphat stood in the assembly of Judah and Jerusalem, in the house of the Lord before the new court, and he said... —2 Chronicles 20:5-6a

1. REMEMBRANCES OF GOD AS ALMIGHTY CREATOR, AND HIS LOVING PROMISES:

1st - REMEMBER THAT GOD REIGNS SUPREMELY OVER
ALL CREATION:
"O LORD, the God of our fathers, are You not God in the heavens? And are You not ruler over all the kingdoms of the nations? Power and might are in Your hand so that no one can stand against You." —2 Chronicles 20:6b

2nd - Remember God's Promises:
*"Did You not, O our God, drive out the inhabitants of this
land before Your people Israel and give it to the
descendants of Abraham Your friend forever? They have
lived in it, and have built You a sanctuary
there for Your name..."* —2 Chronicles 20:7-8

3rd - Remember Your Position as His Child:
*"...saying, 'Should evil come upon us, the sword, or
judgment, or pestilence, or famine, we will stand before this
house and before You (for Your name is in this house) and
cry to You in our distress, and You will
hear and deliver us.'"* —2 Chronicles 20:9

∾

2. State The Problem:

*"Now behold, the sons of Ammon and Moab and Mount Seir,
whom You did not let Israel invade when they came out of the land
of Egypt (they turned aside from them and did not destroy them),
see how they are rewarding us by coming to drive us out from Your
possession which You have given us as an inheritance."*
—2 Chronicles 20:10-11

∾

3. Request Action From Our Father—Key to
answered prayer: Make a humble request & look to
God only for help.

**"O our God, will You not judge them?
For we are powerless before this great multitude
who are coming against us;
nor do we know what to do,
but our eyes are on You."** —2 Chronicles 20:12

ALL JUDAH WAS STANDING BEFORE THE LORD, WITH THEIR INFANTS, their wives and their children. —*2 Chronicles 20:13*

4. GOD ANSWERS JEHOSHAPHAT'S PRAYER THROUGH HIS PROPHET JAHAZIEL:

Then in the midst of the assembly the Spirit of the LORD came upon Jahaziel the son of Zechariah, the son of Benaiah, the son of Jeiel, the son of Mattaniah, the Levite of the sons of Asaph; and he said, "Listen, all Judah and the inhabitants of Jerusalem and King Jehoshaphat: thus says the LORD to you... —*2 Chronicles 20:14-15a*

"...Do not fear or be dismayed because of this great multitude, for the battle is not yours but God's. *Tomorrow go down against them. Behold, they will come up by the ascent of Ziz, and you will find them at the end of the valley in front of the wilderness of Jeruel.*

You need not fight in this battle; station yourselves, stand and see the salvation of the LORD on your behalf, O Judah and Jerusalem.' Do not fear or be dismayed; tomorrow go out to face them, for the Lord is with you." —*2 Chronicles 20:15b-17*

---

5. JEHOSHAPHAT'S RESPONSE WAS TO PRAISE GOD:

Jehoshaphat bowed his head with his face to the ground, and all Judah and the inhabitants of Jerusalem fell down before the LORD, worshiping the LORD. The Levites, from the sons of the Kohathites and of the sons of the Korahites, stood up to praise the LORD God of Israel, with a very loud voice. —*2 Chronicles 20:18-19*

6. THE RESULTS—ENEMIES DESTROY THEMSELVES:

THEY ROSE EARLY IN THE MORNING AND WENT OUT TO THE WILDERNESS OF Tekoa; and when they went out,

Jehoshaphat stood and said, "Listen to me, O Judah and inhabitants of Jerusalem, put your trust in the LORD your God and you will be established. Put your trust in His prophets and succeed."

When he had consulted with the people, he appointed those who sang to the LORD and those who praised Him in holy attire, as they went out before the army and said,

"Give thanks to the LORD,
for His lovingkindness is everlasting."

When they began singing and praising, the LORD set ambushes against the sons of Ammon, Moab and Mount Seir, who had come against Judah; so they were routed. For the sons of Ammon and Moab rose up against the inhabitants of Mount Seir destroying them completely; and when they had finished with the inhabitants of Seir, they helped to destroy one another.

When Judah came to the lookout of the wilderness, they looked toward the multitude, and behold, they were corpses lying on the ground, and no one had escaped.

When Jehoshaphat and his people came to take their spoil, they found much among them, including goods, garments and valuable things which they took for themselves, more than they could carry. And they were three days taking the spoil because there was so much. —2 Chronicles 20:20-25

✝ ✝ ✝

35. FOR A LIFE THAT BLESSES—PRAYER OF JABEZ

There was a man named Jabez who was more honorable than any of his brothers. His mother named him Jabez because his birth had been so painful. He was the one who prayed to the God of Israel. —1 Chronicles 4:9-10a - NLT

"Oh, that you would bless me and expand my territory! Please be with me in all that I do, and keep me from all trouble and pain!" And God granted him his request.

—1 Chronicles 4:10b - NLT

Simple but powerful prayer of Jabez. This is a short, powerful prayer that can be quietly prayed even as one goes about their busy daily schedule.

Certain commentaries have concluded that Jabez requested a pain-free life for himself. However, the Hebrew notion extends the scope of this request to include others. Jabez probably lived with the continuing reminder of the pain he caused his mother. It is thus implied that his plea was that this reputation of causing pain would be reversed. So his prayer was that his life would no longer cause harm or pain for others as well—a humble desire. The circumstances to which we were born do not have to define us.

"With God all things are possible."
—JESUS CHRIST, THE SON OF GOD
(Matthew 19:26)

PRAYER BASED ON 1 CHRONICLES 4:9-10

Oh heavenly Father, I pray that you would bless me and expand my purpose in life that I may be a blessing to others! Please be with me in all that I do, and keep me from all trouble and pain—that my life will be lived in the joy and grace of Your strength, and that I may honor and glorify Your name to all those around me!

MOMENT OF GRATITUDE: I am thankful to have a relationship with You, Lord, to know that with You all things are possible for my life. Following You, keeping my eyes focused on Your grace and love makes me glad throughout my day. Gratitude and feelings of contentment fill my heart as I see You carry out Your purposes for my life!

36. JESUS' FINAL PRAYER—JOHN 17

New Living Translation

*P*ray that what Jesus asked for in His prayer recorded in John 17 is true in your life today. Take note of the special individual requests for His church and ask for awareness of their reality in Your daily life. Prayers and gratitude are shown within Christ's prayer below:

JESUS PRAYER

After saying all these things, Jesus looked up to heaven and said, "Father, the hour has come. Glorify your Son so he can give glory back to you. For you have given him authority over everyone. He gives eternal life to each one you have given him. And this is the way to have eternal life—to know you, the only true God, and Jesus Christ, the one you sent to earth. I brought glory to you here on earth by completing the work you gave me to do. Now, Father, bring me into the glory we shared before the world began." —JOHN 17:1-5

MOMENT OF PRAYER AND GRATITUDE: Dear Heavenly Father, Thank You that I am one of those blessed persons whom You have brought to Jesus. That You have drawn me into a personal friendship with You, and with Jesus Christ who You sent to earth to redeem me. The glory You have revealed to me through Jesus brings me joy. While I ponder that glory You share together as the Triune Godhead, I sit in awesome wonder thinking about those marvelous sights to behold, when at last we all come to be with You eternally!

"I HAVE REVEALED YOU TO THE ONES YOU GAVE ME FROM THIS WORLD. They were always yours. You gave them to me, and they have kept your word. Now they know that everything I have is a gift from you, for I have passed on to them the message you gave me. They accepted it and know that I came from you, and they believe you sent me. My prayer is not for the world, but for those you have given me, because they belong to you. All who are mine belong to you, and you have given them to me, so they bring me glory."
—JOHN 17:6-10

MOMENT OF PRAYER AND GRATITUDE: Lord, thank You for taking me as Your loving possession, and showing me the truth of Your gospel. I pray that I may purpose to bring You glory in my life.

"NOW I AM DEPARTING FROM THE WORLD; THEY ARE STAYING IN THIS world, but I am coming to you. Holy Father, you have given me your name; now protect them by the power of your name so that they will be united just as we are. During my time here, I protected them by

the power of the name you gave me. I guarded them so that not one was lost, except the one headed for destruction, as the Scriptures foretold.

Now I am coming to you. I told them many things while I was with them in this world so they would be filled with my joy. I have given them your word. And the world hates them because they do not belong to the world, just as I do not belong to the world. I'm not asking you to take them out of the world, but to keep them safe from the evil one. They do not belong to this world any more than I do." —JOHN 17:11-16

MOMENT OF PRAYER AND GRATITUDE: Father, please, as Jesus prayed, protect me by the power of Your name that I may live in unity with other believers, and be a "peace-maker" when hatred from the world comes—forgiving quickly any offenses I feel against me. To stand strong and filled with Your joy!

"MAKE THEM HOLY BY YOUR TRUTH; TEACH THEM YOUR WORD, WHICH IS truth. Just as you sent me into the world, I am sending them into the world. And I give myself as a holy sacrifice for them so they can be made holy by your truth.

I am praying not only for these disciples but also for all who will ever believe in me through their message. I pray that they will all be one, just as you and I are one—as you are in me, Father, and I am in you. And may they be in us so that the world will believe you sent me." —JOHN 17:17-21

MOMENT OF PRAYER AND GRATITUDE: Father, as I read Your Word daily, I know You will make me holy in Your truth. Thank You for this promise of Scripture.

Once again, thank You for sending Jesus to be our holy sacrifice.

There is great mystery in me "being" in You, "so that the world will believe You sent Jesus." It is a supernatural type of "dwelling in You", and it is You living through me that the world sees—please let this be true for me today, Father, that Your gospel light will shine brightly through me to others.

"*I HAVE GIVEN THEM THE GLORY YOU GAVE ME, SO THEY MAY BE ONE AS we are one. I am in them and you are in me. May they experience such perfect unity that the world will know that you sent me and that you love them as much as you love me. Father, I want these whom you have given me to be with me where I am. Then they can see all the glory you gave me because you loved me even before the world began!*

O righteous Father, the world doesn't know you, but I do; and these disciples know you sent me. I have revealed you to them, and I will continue to do so. Then your love for me will be in them, and I will be in them." —JOHN 17:22-26

MOMENT OF PRAYER AND GRATITUDE: Father, thank You for the glory that I share with Your Church, in the Person of Jesus Christ. Help us to know Your love even deeper than we have ever experienced before, so the we may have greater understanding of the immense nature of Your love we have through Jesus. May it ever provide us with strength to live together in that same close bond we have with You. That we may experience Your awesome grace, encouragement, love, joy, and peace through one another. Amen.

37. PRAYER OF DAVID FOR A CLEAN CONSCIENCE WHEN TURNING AWAY FROM SIN

New Living Translation

*H*ave mercy on me, O God, because of your unfailing love. Because of your great compassion, blot out the stain of my sins.

> *Wash me clean from my guilt.*
> *Purify me from my sin.*
> *For I recognize my rebellion;*
> *it haunts me day and night.*
>
> *Against you, and you alone, have I sinned;*
> *I have done what is evil in your sight.*
> *You will be proved right in what you say,*
> *and your judgment against me is just.*
>
> *For I was born a sinner— yes,*
> *from the moment my mother conceived me.*
> *But you desire honesty from the womb,*
> *teaching me wisdom even there.*

Purify me from my sins, and I will be clean;
wash me, and I will be whiter than snow.
Oh, give me back my joy again;
you have broken me— now let me rejoice.

Don't keep looking at my sins.
Remove the stain of my guilt.
Create in me a clean heart, O God.
Renew a loyal spirit within me.

Do not banish me from your presence,
and don't take your Holy Spirit from me.
Restore to me the joy of your salvation,
and make me willing to obey you.

Then I will teach your ways to rebels,
and they will return to you.
Forgive me for shedding blood,
O God who saves;
then I will joyfully sing of your forgiveness.

Unseal my lips, O Lord,
that my mouth may praise you.
You do not desire a sacrifice, or I would offer one.
You do not want a burnt offering.

The sacrifice you desire is a broken spirit.
You will not reject a broken and repentant heart, O God.
Look with favor on Zion and help her;
rebuild the walls of Jerusalem.

Then you will be pleased with sacrifices offered in the right spirit—
with burnt offerings and whole burnt offerings.
Then bulls will again be sacrificed on your altar.[1]

Psalm 51 NLT

Prayerful Poetry

Renew me, O eternal Light,
And let my heart and soul be bright,
Illumined with the light of grace
That issues from Your holy face.

Remove the pow'r of sin from me
And cleanse all my impurity
That I may have the strength and will
Temptations of the flesh to still.

Create in me a new heart, Lord,
That gladly I obey Your Word.
Let what You will be my desire,
And with new life my soul inspire.

Grant that I only You may love
And seek those things which are above
Till I behold You face to face,
O Light eternal, through Your grace.

—Johann Friedrich Ruopp, 1714

(Inspired by Psalm 51)

---

1. These types of Old Testament sacrifices point forward to the New Testament initiated by Christ, and represent our 'living sacrifices' in this New Testament era as we take up our cross daily and follow Him.
   See Romans 12:1-2
   and
   *And He was saying to them all, "If anyone wishes to come after Me, he must deny himself, and take up his cross daily and follow Me. —*Luke 9:23

MORNING & EVENING PRAYERS

"I have so much to do that I shall spend the first 3 hours in prayer" –Martin Luther

ENCOURAGEMENT FOR MORNING PRAYER:

It is the proper time to pray
When from sleep awaking;
Ask Him then to be your stay,
In each undertaking;
He would guard you day and night
As your strong Defender,
Unless to Satan's guile and might,
You should then surrender.

Rise with Him at break of day,
Rest in Him while sleeping;
Walk with Jesus on your way,
Happy in His keeping.
—P. FRANK, 1657

I got up early one morning
And rushed right into the day;
I had so much to accomplish
That I didn't have time to pray.

Problems just tumbled about me,
And heavier came each task;
'Why doesn't God help me?' I wondered.
He answered, 'You didn't ask.'

I wanted to see joy and beauty
But the day toiled on gray and bleak;
I wondered why God didn't show me;
He said, "But you didn't seek,"

I tried to come into God's presence;
I used all my keys in the lock.
God gently and lovingly chided,
"My child, you didn't knock."

I woke up early this morning,
And paused before entering the day;
I had so much to accomplish
That I had to take time to pray.

THE DIFFERENCE
—GRACE L. NAESSENS

Encouragement for Evening Prayer:
The day is past and over,
all thanks, O Lord, to thee!
We pray thee that offenseless
the hours of dark may be.
O Jesus, keep us in thy sight,
and guard us through the coming night.

The joys of day are over;
we lift our hearts to thee,
and call on thee that sinless
the hours of dark may be.
O Jesus, make their darkness light,
and guard us through the coming night.

The toils of day are over;
we raise our hymn to thee,
and ask that free from peril
the hours of dark may be.
O Jesus, keep us in thy sight,
and guard us through the coming night.

Be thou our souls' preserver,
O God, for thou dost know
how many are the perils
through which we have to go.
Lord Jesus Christ, O hear our call,
and guard and save us from them all.

—St. Anatolius of Constantinople, 800

(Inspired by - Psalm 13:3)

38. MONDAY—MORNING & EVENING

Moment of Gratitude: Thank you for all the good things that cross my path each day. For my very breath. For the love from others.

Morning — Psalm 5:11-12

I laid me down and slept in peace, and protected by Your mighty hand, I have passed safely through the night. I thank You for this peaceful sleep and Your gracious protection. As I think of all those who are in sorrow, sickness, and pain, I beseech You, the Father of mercies, that You would comfort them with the assurance of Your unchanging grace and loving-kindness. Strengthen my faith and theirs, preserve us from misbelief and despair. Keep me on Your right path and sustain me in Your heavenly kingdom.
In the name of Jesus, Amen.

Evening — Psalm 4:3-8

In this evening hour, I pray, Let the truths of Your Holy Word be precious in my sight, and help me to grow in understanding and knowledge of the Scriptures as I apply their precepts to my own life. Remove from my heart all pride and self-righteousness which might deny my sinful weakness. Keep me throughout the night from every danger, and bless me with peaceful sleep that I may awake refreshed and strengthened to face a new day with all its opportunities to serve You. In Jesus' Name, Amen.

39. TUESDAY—MORNING & EVENING

Moment of Gratitude: Lord, I am grateful that You have redeemed me and called me Your own, that I am Your child forevermore!

Morning —1 Peter 2:11-12

Lord God, thank You for giving me another day, a day to live in Your service and for the good of my neighbors. Please use me for Your glory. By Your Spirit grant me the fitness to work for You this day. I beseech You to make me mindful that I am but a stranger and a pilgrim in this present world. Let me not devote my efforts today to purposes unworthy of You; keep me from every stray path. If I should stumble in sinful weakness, grant me repentance and faith for the sake of Your love. Amen.

Evening —Romans 8:28; 1 Thessalonians 5:12-19

Dear Savior, You have graciously brought me safely to the end of this day. I did not know Your plan for me—what joys or troubles would today be my lot; and now the day is done. Lord, grant that I may view all things that You provided for me as meant for my good. Let me view my successes as encouragements and gifts coming from Your gracious hands. Please protect me this night in peace, that tomorrow I may rise steadfast in faith, abundant in service, warm in love, and unceasing in prayer. You have redeemed me, great God and my Savior; I am Yours. Amen.

40. WEDNESDAY—MORNING & EVENING

Moment of Gratitude: Thank You for the privilege and honor of serving You, even in the small things I do every day.

Morning —Romans 12:1-2; John 13:35

A new day has dawned, my Heavenly Father; as Your child, I turn to You for strength and joy for the day! Let Your love rise in my heart, and let not only my prayer, but my every act, thought, and word, be a sacrifice to You today. Let Your Spirit give me courage and strength to choose the good in every hour. Keep me in oneness of faith and love with my fellow Christians, that together we may be Your light to a darkened world. In Jesus' mighty name I pray, Amen.

Evening —Ephesians 4:17-32

At the close of this day, I come before You in thanksgiving that I have been given another day in which to serve You in the newness of life, purchased for me by the blood of Christ Jesus my Savior. Where I have faltered on the road and grown weary, forgive me. Give me wisdom to be alert to, and strength to reject the allurements of sin. Renew me from this weariness, let Your Word nourish me, Your water of life refresh my parched soul. Grant that I may become more complete in Your holiness — abiding in and with You forever, Amen.

41. THURSDAY—MORNING & EVENING

Moment of Gratitude: I am forever filled with gratitude for Your gift of the Holy Spirit Who comforts and teaches me every moment.

Morning —Luke 12:12; John 14:26

Dear Father in heaven, You have shown me Your loving-kindness by permitting me to rest in peace and to greet, strengthened and refreshed, the light of another day. Let me begin the day with the resolve to serve You. May Your Holy Spirit constantly fill me with love for Your precious Word. Let Him impart to my heart and mind thoughts, words, and deeds which are pleasing in Your sight. As temptations come, help me cling to my blessed Savior. I ask in the name of Jesus Christ, Amen.

Evening —1 John 1:9; 1 Corinthians 2:13

Almighty merciful God, I come before You in this evening hour, exalting You as my Father and Provider. As I look back upon the past hours of this day, I am convicted of my shortcomings. Please forgive me, and refresh my spirit with Your Holy Spirit so that I may withstand and overcome all temptations of unbelief and worldliness. Let Him put pure and wholesome thoughts and desires into my heart. Help all my friends and family who do not know You, that they may come into a saving knowledge of Your truth. Please grant peace and rest to me this night, in Jesus' Name, Amen.

42. FRIDAY–MORNING & EVENING

Moment of Gratitude: Thank You for the hope that I find in Your golden treasury of love and my place reserved in Your glorious heaven.

Morning —Ephesians 5:1-2; 8-14; Matthew 6:19-21

I thank You, my heavenly Father, through Jesus Christ, Your dear Son, that You have kept me safe this night from all danger. I pray that all my "doings" today be pleasing to You, as a sweet-smelling savor. This life is but a vain show; let me not search for an abiding city here. But, Lord, fasten my heart and hope on the life that is in You. Let me not gather treasures for this world; let me not serve mammon, but let my strivings and desires be directed to the treasures of Your love. For Jesus' sake, Amen.

Evening —Ephesians 5:15-21; Philippians 1:21-23

Dear Lord, Let me regard today's perplexities and pains as reminders, chastening, and guidance towards repentance and improvement. The day has gone, O Savior, and I am closer to the hour when I will see You face to face. Let this passing of time make me more ready and watchful for the hour when You come. Let me eagerly prepare myself for Your Day. O Lord, it is better to depart and be with You, yet as long as I am in the land of my pilgrimage, hold my hand; I love You Lord, Amen.

43. SATURDAY—MORNING & EVENING

Moment of Gratitude: I rest in Your arms and am surrounded by Your warm love, grateful for attentive care and guard of Your shepherdry.

Morning -Colossians 2:6-7;Deuteronomy 33:27;Hebrews 12:2-3
Heavenly Father, I am so very thankful for Your love. I ask You to safely lead me through this day. Preserve me in faith. Fill my heart with joy and let me walk with You every hour of this day, honoring Your name by every word I utter and all I do. Uphold me with Your everlasting arms of mercy, and let me not be discouraged by the trials and vexations of the day. Keep Jesus ever before my eyes, let His undying love fill me with a greater love for You, and make me eager to confess Him as my Lord. In His name, Amen.

Evening —Psalm 91; Psalm 119:97
In this evening hour I come to You, merciful Father, thanking You for the goodness and help that You have shown me throughout the day. You have brought me safely home for the night. Make me humble, faithful, thankful. Let nothing be dearer to me than You and Your Word that makes me wise unto salvation. Keep me this night from every danger. Bless me with a quiet, restful sleep. Wherever anxious hearts are lifted up in prayer to You, incline Your ear to them and grant them those things they seek according to Your gracious will. Amen.

44. SUNDAY—MORNING & EVENING

Moment of Gratitude: I thank You that in my community You have established a Christian congregation where Your Word is proclaimed, and for brining me into fellowship with it!

Morning —Psalm 119:103; James 1:22-25
Dear Lord, Your disciples throughout all the world are preparing to assemble to hear Your holy Word and to worship You; please guide everyone safely there, with ears that gladly hear. Keep from my mind distracting thoughts and let Your divine truth be to me more precious than gold and sweeter than honey. Guide me through Your Holy Spirit to be a doer, not just a hearer of Your precious Gospel. Bless my fellow believers and myself for the sake of Your great and merciful love. Amen.

Evening—Proverbs 3:5-8; Romans 8:5-7
Father, I come to You at the close of this Lord's day. Your Word has spoken peace to me in love. As I ponder Your glorious Gospel message, my faith is strengthened. Lead and direct my path, help me walk in Your ways of wisdom this coming week. Thank You for preserving me in the midst of a tempting world and a pleasure-minded people. Let me rest and be refreshed,
I give You all the glory, Amen.

POWERFUL PRAYERS IN ANCIENT HYMNIC POETRY

*Prayer is the soul's sincere desire,
uttered or unexpressed;
the motion of a hidden fire
that trembles in the breast.*

*Prayer is the simplest form of speech
that infant lips can try,
prayer the sublimest strains that reach
the Majesty on high.*

Prayer is the Christian's vital breath,
the Christian's native air,
his watchword at the gates of death:
he enters heaven with prayer.

Prayer is the contrite sinner's voice,
returning from his ways;
while angels in their songs rejoice,
and cry, 'Behold, he prays!

The saints in prayer appear as one,
in word and deed and mind;
while with the Father and the Son
sweet fellowship they find.

Nor prayer is made on earth alone:
the Holy Spirit pleads,
and Jesus on the eternal throne
for sinners intercedes.

O Thou by whom we come to God,
the Life, the Truth, the Way,
the path of prayer thyself hast trod:
Lord, teach us how to pray!

—JAMES MONTGOMERY, 1818

45. DEDICATION TO FOLLOWING GOD—HYMNIC POETRY

READ PRAYERFULLY TO THE LORD WITH GRATITUDE:
TAKE MY LIFE AND USE IT FOR YOUR GLORY
AND MY JOYFUL PRAISE.

Take my life and let it be, consecrated, Lord, to Thee.
Take my moments and my days; let them flow in endless praise.

Take my hands and let them move, at the impulse of Thy love.
Take my feet and let them be, swift and beautiful for Thee.

Take my voice and let me sing, always, only, for my King.
Take my lips and let them be, filled with messages from Thee.

Take my silver and my gold; not a mite would I withhold.
Take my intellect and use, every power as Thou shall choose.

Take my will and make it Yours; it shall be no longer mine.
Take my heart it is thine own; it shall be Thy royal throne.

Take my love; my Lord, I pour, at Thy feet its treasure store.
Take myself, and I will be, ever, only, all for Thee.

—Frances R. Havergal, 1874
(ROMANS 12; ROMANS 6:1-14)

LORD, MAY MY MOUTH EVER HONOR AND PRAISE YOU, TO
DECLARE YOUR HEALING GRACES AND SALVATION.

O for a thousand tongues to sing
my great Redeemer's praise,
the glories of my God and King,
the triumphs of His grace!

Jesus! the name that charms our fears,
that bids our sorrows cease,
'tis music in the sinner's ears,
'tis life and health and peace.

He breaks the power of cancelled sin,
He sets the prisoner free;
His blood can make the foulest clean;
His blood availed for me.

My gracious Master and my God,
assist me to proclaim,
to spread thro' all the earth abroad,
the honors of Your name.

To God all glory, praise, and love
be now and ever given
by saints below and saints above,
the Church in earth and heaven.

—CHARLES WESLEY, 1739
(MATTHEW 26:28; ROMANS 3:25; PSALMS 34:1; 57:7,9; 59:17; 68:4)

46. COMFORT–HYMNIC POETRY

READ PRAYERFULLY TO THE LORD WITH GRATITUDE:
OH LORD, BE MY COMFORT. LET YOUR PRESENCE SURROUND
ME WITH YOUR WARMTH OF LOVE.

Abide with me: fast falls the eventide;
the darkness deepens; Lord, with me abide.
When other helpers fail and comforts flee,
help of the helpless, O abide with me.

I need your presence every passing hour.
What but your grace can foil the tempter's power?
Who like yourself my guide and strength can be?
Through cloud and sunshine, O abide with me.

I fear no foe with you at hand to bless,
though ills have weight, and tears their bitterness.
Where is death's sting? Where, grave, your victory?
I triumph still, if you abide with me.

Hold now your Word before my closing eyes.
Shine through the gloom and point me to the skies.

Heaven's morning breaks and earth's vain shadows flee;
in life, in death, O Lord, abide with me.
HENRY FRANCIS LYTE , 1847

(LUKE 24:29; JOHN 15:1-9; PSALMS 121,123,124,125)

LORD, I SEEK SAFETY IN YOU, MY ROCK AND MY REDEEMER.
My hope is built on nothing less
than Jesus' blood and righteousness;
I dare not trust the sweetest frame,
but wholly lean on Jesus' name.
On Christ, the solid Rock, I stand;
all other ground is sinking sand.

When darkness veils His lovely face,
I rest on His unchanging grace;
in ev'ry high and stormy gale
my anchor holds within the veil.
On Christ, the solid Rock, I stand;
all other ground is sinking sand.

His oath, His covenant, His blood
support me in the 'whelming flood;
when all around my soul gives way
He then is all my hope and stay.
On Christ, the solid Rock, I stand;
all other ground is sinking sand.

When He shall come with trumpet sound,
O may I then in Him be found,
dressed in His righteousness alone,
faultless to stand before the throne.
On Christ, the solid Rock, I stand;
all other ground is sinking sand.
—EDWARD MOTE , 1834

(Proverbs 10:22; Psalm 18; psalm 19:4)

47. LOVE & ADMIRATION FOR GOD—HYMNIC POETRY

READ PRAYERFULLY TO THE LORD WITH GRATITUDE:
LORD JESUS MY LOVING AND ETERNAL SAVIOR, YOUR NAME
IS PRECIOUS TO ME.

*How sweet the name of Jesus sounds
in a believer's ear!
It soothes our sorrows, heals our wounds,
and drives away our fear.*

*It makes the wounded spirit whole
and calms the troubled breast;
'tis manna to the hungry soul,
and to the weary, rest.*

*O Jesus, shepherd, guardian, friend,
my Prophet, Priest, and King,
my Lord, my Life, my Way, my End,
accept the praise I bring.*

How weak the effort of my heart,
how cold my warmest thought;
but when I see you as you are,
I'll praise you as I ought.

Till then I would your love proclaim
with every fleeting breath;
and may the music of your name
refresh my soul in death.

—JOHN NEWTON, 1779

(ISAIAH 9:6; 53:4-5; 61:1-4; REVELATION 19:13,16;

SONG OF SOLOMON 4:16; PSALM 25; 31:23-24; 66:4)

∽

LORD JESUS I STAND IN WONDER AT YOUR BEAUTY, IT IS
GREATER THAN THE FINEST TREASURES OF SKY AND EARTH. I
AM STRENGTHENED JUST BY PONDERING IT.

Beautiful Savior, King of creation,
Son of God and Son of Man!
Truly I'd love Thee, truly I'd serve thee,
Light of my soul, my Joy, my Crown.

Fair are the meadows, Fair are the woodlands,
Robed in flow'rs of blooming spring;
Jesus is fairer, Jesus is purer;
He makes our sorr'wing spirit sing.

Fair is the sunshine, Fair is the moonlight,
Bright the sparkling stars on high;
Jesus shines brighter, Jesus shines purer
Than all the angels in the sky.

Beautiful Savior, Lord of the nations,
Son of God and Son of Man!
Glory and honor, Praise, adoration,
Now and forevermore be Thine!

—AUTHOR UNKNOWN, DATE UNKNOWN

(PSALM 45, ISAIAH 61:10; 62.5)

~

MY FATHER, THANK YOU FOR THE PRIVILEGE OF COMING
BEFORE YOU IN YOUR HOLY PLACE. LET MY LIFE SHINE IN
PRAISE & GLORIOUS SERVICE.

Open now Thy gates of beauty, Zion, let me enter there,
where my soul in joyful duty waits for God who answers prayer.
O how blessed is this place, filled with solace, light, and grace.

Gracious God, I come before Thee; come Thou also unto me,
where we find Thee & adore Thee, there a heaven on earth must be.
To my heart O enter Thou; let it be Thy temple now.

Here Thy praise is gladly chanted, here Thy seed is duly sown.
Let my soul, where it is planted, bring forth precious sheaves alone.
So that all I hear may be, fruitful unto life in me.

Thou my faith increase and quicken, let me keep Thy gift divine.
Howsoe'er temptations thicken; may Your Word still o'er me shine.
As my guiding star through life, as my comfort in my strife.

Speak, O Lord, and I will hear Thee; let Thy will be done indeed,
may I undisturbed draw near Thee, while Thou dost Thy people feed.
Here of life the fountain flows; here is balm for all our woes.

—BENJAMIN SCHMOLCK, 1704
(PSALM 24:7-10; 27:4-6; 63: 1-8; 100; 1 CORINTHIANS 6:19-20)

48. STRONGER FAITH—HYMNIC POETRY

READ PRAYERFULLY TO THE LORD WITH GRATITUDE;
FATHER, I DESIRE A PURE FAITH IN YOU, A FAITH THAT
TRUSTS NO MATTER WHAT...

O for a faith that will not shrink,
Though pressed by many a foe,
That will not tremble on the brink
Of any earthly woe,

That will not murmur nor complain
Beneath the chast'ning rod,
But in the hour of grief or pain
Will lean upon its God.

A faith that shines more bright and clear
When tempests rage without,
That, when in danger, knows no fear,
In darkness feels no doubt,

That bears unmoved the world's dread frown,
Nor heeds its scornful smile,
That seas of trouble cannot drown,
Nor Satan's arts beguile,

A faith that keeps the narrow way
Till life's last hour is fled,
And with a pure and heav'nly ray
Lights up a dying bed.

Lord, give us such a faith as this,
And then, whate'er may come,
We'll taste e'en here the hallowed bliss
Of an eternal home.

—WILLIAM HILEY BATHURST, 1831

(LUKE 17:5)

49. PRAISE & WORSHIP—HYMNIC POETRY

READ PRAYERFULLY TO THE LORD WITH GRATITUDE:
IT IS MY GREATEST HONOR TO PRAISE YOU.

All hail the power of Jesus' name! Let angels prostrate fall.
Bring forth the royal diadem, and crown Him Lord of all!

O seed of Israel's chosen race, now ransomed from the fall,
hail Him who saves you by his grace, and crown Him Lord of all!

Let every nation, every tribe, on this terrestrial ball,
to Him all majesty ascribe, and crown Him Lord of all!

Oh, that with all the sacred throng, we at His feet may fall!
We'll join the everlasting song, and crown Him Lord of all!

—EDWARD PERRONET, 1780
(REVELATION 19:12;16; 21:22-27)

LORD, HELP MY MIND FOCUS ON YOU THROUGHOUT MY DAY,
LET ME SPEAK PRAISES TO YOU.

Praise to the LORD, the Almighty, the King of creation!
O my soul, praise Him, for He is thy health and salvation.
All ye who hear, now to His temple draw near:
join me in glad adoration!

Praise to the LORD, who o'er all things so wondrously reigneth,
shelters thee under His wings, yea, so gently sustaineth!
Hast thou not seen - how thy desires e'er have been
granted in what He ordaineth?

Praise to the LORD, who with marvelous wisdom hath made thee,
decked thee with health, & with loving hand guided & stayed thee.
How oft in grief - hath not He brought thee relief,
spreading His wings for to shade thee!

Praise to the LORD, who doth prosper thy works and defend thee;
surely His goodness and mercy here daily attend thee.
Ponder anew - what the Almighty can do,
if with His love He befriend thee.

Praise to the LORD, O let all that is in me adore Him!
All that hath life and breath, come now with praises before Him!
Let the amen - sound from His people again:
gladly forever adore Him!

—Joachim Neander, 1680

(NEHEMIAH 9:6; PSALM 103:1-7; 104)

50. FOR NEW YEAR—HYMNIC POETRY

Read Prayerfully to the Lord with gratitude:
Lord, a new year is beginning. Eternal Father, be my
guide as I step closer to the time I will be with You
for eternity.

Our God, our Help in ages past,
our Hope for years to come,
our Shelter from the stormy blast,
and our eternal Home.

Under the shadow of Thy throne
Thy saints have dwelt secure;
sufficient is Thine arm alone,
and our defense is sure.

Before the hills in order stood
or earth received its frame,
from everlasting Thou art God,
to endless years the same.

A thousand ages in Thy sight
are like an ev'ning gone,
short as the watch that ends the night
before the rising sun.

Time, like an ever-rolling stream,
bears all its sons away;
they fly forgotten, as a dream
dies at the op'ning day.

Our God, our Help in ages past,
our Hope for years to come,
be Thou our Guide while life shall last,
and our eternal Home!

—Isaac Watts, 1719

(Psalm 90:1-6;12-17)

❧

Jesus, I invite You into my planning and goals.
My 'best life now' is in the path
You divinely place before me.

Help us, O Lord, for now we enter
Upon another year today.
In you our hopes and thoughts now center;
Renew our courage for the way.
New life, new strength, new happiness
We ask of you -- oh, hear and bless.

May ev'ry plan and undertaking
Begin this year, O Lord, with you;
When I am sleeping or am waking,
Help me, dear Lord, your will to do.
In you alone, my God, I live;
You only can my sins forgive.

And may this year to me be holy;
Your grace so fill my ev'ry thought
That all my life be pure and lowly
And truthful, as a Christian's ought.
So make me while I'm living here
Your faithful servant through the year.

Jesus, be with me and direct me;
Jesus, my plans and hopes inspire;
Jesus, from tempting thoughts protect me;
Jesus, be all my heart's desire;
Jesus, be in my thoughts all day
And never let me fall away.

And grant, Lord, when the year is over,
That it for me in peace may close.
In all things care for me and cover
My head in time of fear and woes.
So may I, when my life is done,
Appear with joy before your throne.

—JOHANN RIST , 1644

(ROMANS 12; PSALM 90:12,17; ISAIAH 40:28-31; JOSHUA 1:8-9; JEREMIAH 29:11)

PRAYER OF BLESSING FOR YOU

Prayer For You - Beloved in Christ

May our Lord and Shepherd keep you safe in the
pastures of His loving care. May He feed you with the
heavenly food that provides growth and strength, and
surround You with His presence as you tread in places
of trouble.

We will meet some day in that lovely place where the
Sun of Light shines evermore. Until then, may He
continually shine His face upon you and keep you
in peace.

In the Name of our Great Savior, Jesus Christ
Amen

Ancient Irish Blessings

May God give you...
For every storm a rainbow,
For every tear a smile,
For every care a promise,
And a blessing in each trial.
For every problem life sends,
A faithful friend to share,
For every sigh a sweet song,
And an answer for each prayer.

God Bless You Eternally

Made in United States
Troutdale, OR
08/01/2024

21687566R00101